**Love Me, Love My Dog
Complete Dog Ownership Manual**

TS-212

Facing page: A prize pair of Cocker Spaniel puppies. Right: Am. Ch. Topsham Rainbow Tapestry, left: Topsham Rainbow Finale, TD, WD owned by Carol B. Richter and Llana K. Comini. Photo by Jerry Vavra.

Overleaf: CHILDREN AND DOGS. Little girl with Dachshund photographed by Susan Miller.

Distributed in the UNITED STATES to the Pet Trade by T.F.H. Publications, Inc., One T.F.H. Plaza, Neptune City, NJ 07753; distributed in the UNITED STATES to the Bookstore and Library Trade by National Book Network, Inc. 4720 Boston Way, Lanham MD 20706; in CANADA to the Pet Trade by H & L Pet Supplies Inc., 27 Kingston Crescent, Kitchener, Ontario N2B 2T6; Rolf C. Hagen Ltd., 3225 Sartelon Street, Montreal 382 Quebec; in CANADA to the Book Trade by Macmillan of Canada (A Division of Canada Publishing Corporation), 164 Commander Boulevard, Agincourt, Ontario M1S 3C7; in ENGLAND by T.F.H. Publications, PO Box 15, Waterlooville PO7 6BQ; in AUSTRALIA AND THE SOUTH PACIFIC by T.F.H. (Australia), Pty. Ltd., Box 149, Brookvale 2100 N.S.W., Australia; in NEW ZEALAND by Brooklands Aquarium Ltd. 5 McGiven Drive, New Plymouth, RD1 New Zealand; in Japan by T.F.H. Publications, Japan—Jiro Tsuda, 10-12-3 Ohjidai, Sakura, Chiba 285, Japan; in SOUTH AFRICA by Multipet Pty. Ltd., P.O. Box 35347, Northway, 4065, South Africa. Published by T.F.H. Publications, Inc.
MANUFACTURED IN THE UNITED STATES OF AMERICA
BY T.F.H. PUBLICATIONS, INC.

LOVE ME, LOVE MY DOG
COMPLETE DOG OWNERSHIP MANUAL

Barry Carruthers, M.D. and Keith Bing MBIPDT

Contents

CONTENTS

PUPPY LOVE. Puppies bring out a child's personality, often giving the child confidence and self-assurance. This evocative tyke is a Sloughi puppy. Photo by E. Moreau-Sipiére.

Dedications

This book is dedicated to the dogs we have loved so dearly and who have loved us: "Hustler" Bing, "Warden" Buckley, Archbishop Carey's "Duke of Buccleuch," "Rufus" Carruthers, "Rollo" Chapman, "Rudi" Combe, "Heidi" Gailey, "Sable" Horn, "Topaz" Llewellyn, "Jodi" Rose and "Camilla" Waley.

Acknowledgements

To Gill Bing, a very special thanks for without her dedication, organisation and typing skills this book would not have been possible.

The authors would like to thank the many individuals and organisations who contributed so enthusiastically to this book, lending it depth in many of their specialised subjects.

Special thanks are due to Archbishop of Canterbury (The Most Rev. Dr. George Carey), Inger Chapman, Richard Croft, Göran Heyman, John Nicol MRCVS, David Sampson, Hilary Self and His Honour Judge A.F. Waley VRD, QC, DL, for their contributions; Lorraine Gailey BSSc, Ph.D., as consultant on psychiatry and psychology; Lynette Hart Ph.D., for her help on companion animal studies; Elizabeth Abbott BVMS, Ph.D., MRCVS, for technical support; Jane Rose BVMS, MRCVS and her colleague Simone Vitale BVMS (Murd), for the Australian input; Gerard Evans of *Today* newspaper.

We are grateful to Betty Chadwick, James Combe, Graeme of Eastbourne, Ralph Hutchings and Derek Tamea, for their photography; to Gyn Horn, for her illustrations and for their patience in dealing with our many requests; also to the Rev. Wallace Boulton, for help in proofreading.

Our thanks to the following: Bailey & Mathewson MsRCVS, The British Institute of Professional Dog Trainers, Blue Cross Animal Welfare, the City of Perth Health Department, Great Ormond Street Hospital for Sick Children, Hoechst Animal Health, J. Hudson & Co. (Whistles) Limited, the Ministry of Agriculture, Fisheries and Food (UK), the National Canine Defence League, *Pet Dogs* magazine, the School of Veterinary Medicine— University of California, Trekök-Doggy AB (Sweden) and the World Health Organisation.

Also to our unsung heroes: Malcolm Barton with "Asta," "Sabre" and "Kira"; Dave Thompson, for his wonderful shepherding skills, and his dog "Sam"; and our computer wizard Doug Eaton.

Foreword

By Tom Buckley
General Secretary and Registrar, British Institute of Professional Dog Trainers

When I embarked on a career in dog training around 1948, dog ownership was somewhat different than it is today. Contagious diseases like distemper and the newly arrived hard pad were prevalent with no means of immunisation. Little was known about dog nutrition, although this was not of great concern as finding dog food of any kind was a constant problem. There were few dog training clubs as those that had been in existence prior to the War were just starting to establish themselves again. A handful of trainers who had learned their trade in the services had started modest training kennels.

There was, of course, no necessity for dog wardens and in the legislative field no hastily cobbled together Guard Dogs Act or the equally contentious Dangerous Dogs Act. Above all was the non-existence of a highly organised and vocal anti-dog lobby.

Very few books on dog training or related subjects had been written. Those that were available either dealt with it in very general terms or were devoted to a particular breed.

Over the past few years there has been a proliferation of books published on the many facets of dog ownership, training and its various elements. I am often asked for advice on suitable books and find no difficulty in giving this if it is on a specific subject. What I have found is the absence of what I would describe as a compendium of up-to-date information that would act as a reference book for the caring owner.

In this erudite and yet easily read book I think my quandary has been solved.

Introduction

A family dog, a show dog, a working dog, a guard dog—or just a companion—a dog can be all these things but the way it is managed from the start determines your success as a dog owner. The initial step is to choose the right type of dog to suit your needs and circumstances and to learn how to obtain one. Then it has to be properly trained and cared for to ensure that it becomes a healthy, enjoyable companion for your household and safe for others. The team of a veterinarian, professional dog trainer/ behaviourist and a medical doctor, together with advice from

Barry Carruthers, M.D., co-author. Photo by R. Hutchings.

Geoffrey Llewellyn, BVSc, MRCVS, veterinary advisor. Photo by R. Hutchings.

a high court judge on the law and the owner of a highly successful boarding kennel on this subject, covers all of these aspects plus how to cope with any problems that may arise. There are many breeds and mixtures of breeds of dogs, each with individual characteristics. All start as adorable little puppies, but they soon grow up and show their inbred features. They may become very large or need a lot of exercise. Some are patient with children or suitable for training as working dogs. Most offer loyalty and trust for the whole of their lives and in return their owners must accept the responsibility of total care and control.

The dog is a social animal that needs love, companionship and stimulation, without which it will get into trouble like a neglected child.

Problems of illness or behaviour can occur and, naturally, all dogs age. These areas are fully covered by the respective specialists.

It is the front and rear ends of the dog that have to be trained and looked after, whilst a careful eye is kept on the coat in between.
BARRY CARRUTHERS, M.D.

Keith Bing, MBIPDT, co-author and compiler, with German Shepherd Dog, Inca, and Briard, Sam. Photo by J. Combe.

Love Me, Love My Dog

Undoubtedly there is something pleasantly infectious about animals as company, and once the habit is formed a home seems lonely without some form of pet around. Affection is bred early when young children want something personal they can care for and play with, and usually first choice is a small fry they can handle, such as a hamster, gerbil or even a mouse. From this beginning a lifetime urge for animal companionship is acquired, and later preference often matches the particular pets with which they grew up at home.

A policeman friend, who bred Alsatians in his back garden as a hobby, had three sons and a daughter, each of whom in turn chose their first pet. The elder lad followed in his father's footsteps and picked an Alsatian pup, going on in time to breed pedigrees in a big way. The second opted for goldfish, which became an obsession that dominated his life—and that of his own family. Whenever they moved, the new house had to have garden space for a pond to hold his Japanese koi carp and a garage large enough to house his tropical fish. The third son started with a budgie and became a well-known breeder of racing pigeons! Not to be outdone, his daughter chose a white rabbit which she called Peter. Far from proving tame, Peter turned out to be more aggressive and dangerous than any of the Alsatians. He would

burrow out of his run and attack any dog or person in sight, biting their legs or ankles and driving them, yelping, indoors. Only the girl could control him and she would come home from school to find the family had shut themselves in the house with Peter in unchallenged control of the whole garden. To add to the dogs' trouble, the lady next door kept a mynah bird which learned to mimic to perfection the wife's voice and the commands she would shout at the dogs. They would run out into the garden when the bird called out "Come" to find no one there. Mealtimes became chaotic when the wife would call "Good boys—dinner" with no response, only to find them obediently lying on the ground to the mynah's screeches of "Down" and "Stay".

More than half the houses in Britain have at least one pet, outnumbering televisions in the United States. Cats and dogs are well ahead in the popularity league because they live in as part of the family, but goldfish and caged birds are also popular. The balance in choice has changed with the pattern of living as more couples go out to work and own their own home, which, with the urban sprawl, means an apartment or house with a small garden and limited access to open spaces. The resultant trend has been towards pets that can be kept in a cage or bowl or can be independent during the day, such as cats and smaller dogs that may need less exercise.

As so many people enjoy animal company, it is inevitable that their motivation should be analysed in depth and attempts made to measure the benefits. The result has been a flood of literature in recent years from veterinarians, psychologists and even the medical profession, the vast majority of which has supported the fact that pet ownership satisfies some basic human needs and plays a positive part towards a happier and even healthier life. The build up of interest and research into the true value of the role of the pet in both personal and family relationships has led

LOVE ME, LOVE MY DOG. Despite his large size, the Great Dane generally has a kind and gentle nature and can make an ideal companion for children of all ages. Photo by R. Hutchings.

to a great change in attitudes towards owners. Before it was accepted as a natural phase for children to want pets as playthings, a stage they would grow out of. Continuation into adult life was regarded at best with tolerant amusement and at worst as a sign of immaturity and a substitute for adult human relationships or for children.

Now the real benefits are being evaluated for all ages and stages of life events from childhood to later years. Response to pets' company can start early—within a year babies will prefer a warm, cuddly pet to a furry toy and may learn to say "cat" or "dog" before "mum" or "dad". This friendship is followed through with great benefit by young children, who will often treat their pet as best friend or communicant. The need to look after a pet and play with it can encourage the development of many positive traits that we like to see in our children, and it helps them to become less self-centred and more caring and friendly towards other children and adults. It is through their pets that they can come to terms with the facts of life, such as sex, birth and even death, whilst teenage owners have been found to be more popular and sociable with their peers.

It is later in life that the greatest value has been shown. Ask the average owner why he keeps a pet and he will say that it

THE FACTS OF LIFE. Taking care of a dog can teach a child much about birth, reproduction and even death. Photo by S. Camp.

HAPPY BIRTHDAY! More and more people are beginning to treat their dogs like one of the family. Photo by A. Jaksic.

is the pleasure of the pet's company. Psychologically speaking, this is because it is helping to fulfill certain basic human needs for life satisfaction such as to love and be loved, to be accepted and respected as a person, to have others depend on them and to know there is a worthwhile purpose in life.

Ideally these needs are satisfied within a family background where one can relax from the stresses of work and everyday life and pets are a "top-up" that all can enjoy. But for many, particularly older people, life events dictate that their pets play a bigger role to replace loss of interests and combat loneliness.

Families are smaller and more concentrated. Retirement—or early redundancy—and children leaving home to live together long before they get married break down the familiar schedules that regulate life. It may be a relief not to have to drive to work or take the children to school, but the free time has to be taken up by both partners. Hobbies such as golf and gardening, social clubs and voluntary work are fine, but there is still a gap at home to be filled to build up a new comradeship. The companionship of a pet or two around the house can be a great comfort and be a new lifeline both can enjoy and look after.

There has been a great deal of study on the contribution that pets can make to the quality of life for older people who can easily become isolated and pre-occupied with themselves and their ailments. Some may have little else of interest to take up their time and minds. Although difficult to prove on a strictly scientific basis, there is considerable evidence that pet owners live happier, healthier and even longer lives and can weather stressful events, such as bereavement, more readily. The benefits show up in many ways. The need to care for the pet maintains a pattern to life and offers an outlet for affection at home. Owners are more relaxed and companionable for others and have more friends and visitors. Their dependence on tranquilisers for depression and sedatives to sleep is less and it has even been shown that the chance of surviving a heart attack is much greater.

Most of these reports relate to dogs and cats, but even goldfish have been shown to be of value. A bowl of goldfish in the bedroom of elderly residents at an old folks home ensured visitors stayed much longer, even after the grapes had been eaten!

Personal preferences for cats or dogs are deep-rooted and argument about their respective values can lead to stronger feelings than the battle of the sexes. Kittens and puppies start life on equal terms as adorable fluffy little playthings, but they soon grow their separate ways. The cat becomes an independent-minded animal that is more territorial than family-minded. It can look after itself during the day and come back in the evening for warmth, comfort and companionship. It is therefore an ideal pet for those at work and for seniors in apartments as it leads a quiet life that does not disturb neighbours.

A dog stays a total dependent who needs a home with a master and accepts family and friends as part of a pack to which it stays loyal and will not be seduced by comfort elsewhere. The relationship between the owner and his or her dog is therefore a more intimate affair and the dog is a personal companion outdoors as well as at home. Their greeting is passionate with a total body language that shows "welcome" from tip to tail, which can be embarrassing or even frightening to non-doggy types, especially by large dogs who seem to have an inherent urge to explore nose-first the areas that are usually regarded as "private". The depth of affection that the owners of all ages feel was well shown by the response to a request in a leading dog magazine for photographs for this book. Every contribution was accompanied by a letter showing how much their pet meant and many of these pets had been taken on from rescue homes. People can seem as single-minded and boring about their pets as about their children, but at least they can be a more interesting source of conversation than the weather and one's aches and pains.

VARIETY IS THE SPICE OF LIFE. There are many different types of dogs for many different types of people. Choose a dog that best fits your personality and lifestyle. Photo by N. Stokes.

The discipline that a dog can be taught together with natural sociability means that it can be trained as a safe outdoor companion with great benefits for all concerned. If you watch an old lady escorted by her dog to the shops, she will meet on her way many people who stop for a chat with her and a pat for the dog. This mutual bond can be common ground for many friendships and open up communication at all ages and stages of life.

This is especially evident for the elderly and physically or mentally handicapped who have to enter sheltered housing or residential care. Often all pets are banned, although it has been shown that pets can bring pleasure and higher morale for the residents. Since 1983 California federal law has protected the rights of seniors and handicapped people in rented housing to own pets and, under the banner "Housing Happy Pets and Happy People," lays down guidelines for tenants and management to ensure lack of nuisance for others with great success. In the few hospitals where communal residential pets have been allowed, the relationship between staff and patients has been improved and in prisons the level of violence has been reduced.

Realisation of the pleasure and comfort their pets can bring has brought thousands of dog owners together to share them with others who cannot enjoy a personal pet and a visiting scheme has been set up for the elderly and handicapped. Under the title "Pets as Therapy" (U.K. and Australia, "Therapy Pets" in the U.S.A.), the organisation has become international with assistance dogs visiting patients at home, in hospitals and in prisons.

The discipline that dogs can acquire from proper training has been put to many helpful purposes, and it is their nature to become eyes for the blind or ears for the deaf. In Holland they have even been trained to look after the disabled who are confined to a wheelchair, learning to fetch and carry at home or when they go shopping—although personally I have never been able to teach

MY BEST FRIEND. Dogs are welcomed visitors at many hospitals and nursing homes. Here, a resident looks forward to spending time with his canine friend. Photo by G. Gibbs.

COMPANION...IN NEED. Well-disciplined dogs can be trained to assist the blind, deaf and disabled. Photo by G. Gibbs.

mine to fetch my slippers, morning paper or flask of brandy when I feel like a drink.

The natural instincts of a dog give it many other roles to play apart from a mere companion. It brings a sense of security and protection into the home. The police accept a dog as a better safeguard than any flashing lights or burglar alarm. On a station platform recently I watched a family with their two Rottweilers safely on leads, obviously mother and daughter. They lay down quietly to order until the two children went off to the buffet to get a cola. The dogs at once became restless and watched the buffet door like hawks until the children came back, when they settled down again.

Your Commitment to a New Pet

Your new puppy will probably become your best friend but it may not always feel like this when he or she wakes you at 3 a.m., messes on your new carpet or refuses to come when called. Like babies, puppies enter this world without social graces or discipline but, as with children, love and firmness should conquer all and every ounce of effort will be rewarded many times over in the lifelong relationship with your best friend.

THE RESCUE DOG

It is likely that the rescued dog has had a pretty raw deal throughout its life. It will certainly have been through the trauma of having to leave its mother, going to a new home, having settled in there and being shunted off to a kennel to be re-homed yet again. With some unfortunate dogs this may have happened several times. *THERE CAN BE NO GREATER REWARD THAN A SUCCESSFUL RE-HOMING OF A RESCUED DOG, MANY OF WHICH MAKE THE MOST LOYAL AND LOVING COMPANIONS.* However, please think long and hard when rescuing a dog. Very often they do come with behavioural problems possibly the cause of their re-housing in the first place. Whether you buy a puppy or rescue a more mature dog, be resolute that you see the difficult periods through to a happy conclusion. We don't send our children back if they don't match up to our expectations, so why consider the same with your dog?

Consider these slogans: *A Dog*

I'M YOURS—FOREVER. Rescue dogs make wonderful pets, which are extremely appreciative and responsive to your love and care. Photo by T.B. Chadwick.

I NEED A HOME. Many dogs end up in shelters because people buy dogs on whims. Make sure you consider the whole commitment before acquiring a dog. Photo by T.B. Chadwick.

Is For Life, Not Just For Christmas issued by National Canine Defence League, U.K.

Dogs Deserve Better People issued by PRO Dogs, U.K.

A Dog Is A Ten Year Partnership issued by The Blue Cross Animal Welfare, U.K.

THE ENVIRONMENT FACTOR

Having made your commitment to buy a new puppy or to rescue a dog, first study your surroundings.

What size dwelling?

There is no reason why a flat/apartment dweller or somebody living in a mobile home should not equally enjoy the pleasure of canine partnership but a Great Dane, for example, may prove a problem in such a confined area.

Are you house-proud?

Golden Retrievers are certainly beautiful dogs but how will you feel when they moult all over your new velour three-piece suite?

Your new puppy may have accidents, wetting or messing on your Persian carpet. How cross would you be by such behaviour?

Supposing your Dalmatian, with one swipe of its tail, devastated your Ming vase?

Are you garden-proud?

You may have spent many years nurturing your lovely garden. A dog can devastate it in a fraction of the time it took you to grow it! Your beautiful lawn, once admired by visitors, may suddenly develop white patches when a dog enters your life and your garden. Is your garden secure? You may have acres of land justifiably thinking this would make an ideal environment for a dog but is it possible or practical to secure this area?

Perhaps you live in the country surrounded by sheep or cattle. Consider your breed. Some just adore the "thrill of the chase".

Where can I take my dog for a walk?

Even if you have a large amount of land on which to exercise your dog, it is still desirable that your dog is taken to places of recreation to alleviate boredom and allow social interaction with other dogs and people. Do you have such places available to you?

Are you a natty dresser?

The Afghan Hound may well grace your home, but it may be that you work in a city office, donning an immaculate dark suit. How will you feel when your dog deposits its coat on your coat as you leave in the morning? Do you have smart dinner parties? A Dobermann taken to the front door will certainly deter the unwanted visitor, but the same dog leaping over your newly arrived guests will cause the evening to be a disaster!

WORK

Are you and your family out to work all day or perhaps the husband is working and the wife has a busy schedule ferrying children to school, possibly combined with a part-time job and regular social activity? You will acquire your dog for the pleasure of his company. He too will enjoy the pleasure of your company. Is it therefore fair to leave him locked up alone indoors for eight hours a day? A puppy in particular will require almost continual company and guidance. Will you be quite patient and tolerant when you return one day to find your rubbish bins emptied, your kitchen units chewed and wet patches on the floor, or will your puppy get the attention it

THE HAIR OF THE DOG. The length of a dog's coat is a big consideration for potential owners. Long-haired dogs mean lots of grooming and shedding. Photo by R. Hutchings.

needs?

OTHER ANIMALS

It may be that you will bring a young puppy to the home of an older dog. This would normally result in a new lease on life for your old chum. Consider, however, how fair it is for the aged Labrador suffering from severe arthritis being pummeled by a young and naturally playful puppy. It is not unusual for dogs and cats to have a love/hate relationship. Dogs love to chase cats and cats hate it! How will your cats fare with this sudden intrusion into their lives?

Many breeds are of a more predatory nature and may well kill a pet rabbit, guinea pig or chickens. Will suitable arrangements be made for your other animals to be secure?

CHILDREN

The joy of our children growing up with dogs and learning to love and respect them is immeasurable, as is the joy that children give to dogs.

But are your children going to respect your dog's feelings or are they more likely to pull his ears and tail? Are your children quite calm or are they likely to run around shrieking and over-

A FAMILY FRIEND. Children should be taught to love and respect a dog as they would a person, perhaps even more. Photo by R. Hutchings.

A ROMP ON THE BEACH. Owners must find time to exercise their dogs daily. Make sure that large dogs have plenty of wide open space so that they may enjoy a good run. Photo by P. Aze.

exciting your dog?

Conversely are you thinking of obtaining a guarding dog who may well not be of suitable character for a young family?

THE PREGNANT MOTHER

Is it possible that your puppy will take a back seat as soon as the baby is born? Will you change and become over-protective towards your new child? Indeed will granny become over-protective?

THE OLDER OWNER

Many of us say in our young and middle ages that we will never have another dog when we reach mature years but who can deny the infinite pleasure a dog can give to the older owner who will certainly have the time and love to offer. But how will you feel when your newly acquired rescued Lurcher decides to take to the woods for a bit of hunting? What if your delightfully placid Labrador turns out to be not so placid, maybe pulling you along the road, not realising you have a back condition?

THE FIRST-TIME OWNER

We all have to start somewhere and our thought for the first-time owner is "you don't know what a pleasure you've been missing" but do consider the changes to your lifestyle. You may be awakened late at night whilst your puppy is settling in, you will have to find time to exercise, train and play with your dog and you will need to make arrangements when going away on holiday. Will you mind these changes?

THE EXPERIENCED OWNER

Your last dog was probably the apple of your eye, otherwise you would not be considering another one, but please be patient whilst your new acquisition enters your heart and learns your expectations. How many of us forget after say fourteen years that even our "perfect" dog may once have been a "pain"!

THE EXPENSE

Dogs are not relatively expensive in terms of food, bedding and equipment, but for the unlucky owner a sick dog can produce expensive veterinary bills. Will you have the money for such bills or are you planning on

THE COST OF CARING. Along with the normal costs that come with owning a dog, allow room in your budget for unforeseen expenses, such as kenneling or medical emergencies. Photo by R. Hutchings.

pet insurance, which itself would be additional expense? Other expenses to allow for will be yearly inoculations, six-monthly worming, kenneling during your holiday and professional grooming for dogs who require this.

ANXIETY ABOUT YOUR PREVIOUS DOG

Perhaps your previous dog may have tragically slipped the leash and been run over. Maybe he was very aggressive towards other dogs or even your children. You were probably just unlucky; even the fact that you are reading this book suggests that you are trying not to let history repeat itself. You are doubtlessly a much wiser owner.

TWO DOGS (OR MORE)

Many people buy two dogs so that they may be company for each other. This is a perfectly reasonable judgement. However, you cannot always assume that two or more dogs will necessarily get on with one another. Another dog is not a substitute for its human partner. Remember dogs tend to learn more naughty things from other dogs than good things!

We have tried to point out in this section some of the points that potential owners may not be aware of that may lead to annoyance, anger and possible re-homing of the new dog. Remember it is easy to be wise after the event but in no way do we wish to discourage you from the joy and love a dog can bring into your life.

BUDDIES. This group of Cocker Spaniels gets along well with one another, an important characteristic for multi-dog households. Photo by T. Lamb.

Reassurance to the Worried New Owner

A well-trained dog that is properly cared for is one of the safest of pets. Others can be far more dangerous to their owners and the public at large. Cats, for example, may spread the parasite that causes toxoplasmosis (should infection occur early in the mother's pregnancy, the result may be loss of her baby, blindness or nervous damage to the child later in life). There are no exceptions amongst pets. Parrots and pigeons can pass on a serious form of pneumonia, tame white mice and rabbits can house tapeworms, and hamsters can pass on meningitis.

All pets can be involved in food poisoning and even turtles and terrapins have caused salmonella outbreaks. Dogs and cats come closest to us and are therefore potentially the most dangerous. They are a favourite home for worms and can pick up many other infections. However, a well trained dog can be controlled more than any other pet by a responsible owner to minimise its potential dangers. From time to time there are big scares that highlight these dangers, but they must be kept in proportion. There

WHO ME? Dogs make loyal pets who love their owners unconditionally. Photo by A. Chen.

MY COMFORT ZONE. A well-treated, well-trained dog makes a happy, disciplined pet—a pleasure for any household. Photo by Z. Skivington.

are more than seven million dogs in the U.K. and over 52 million in the U.S.A., but serious problems are rare. Let us put aside the minimal health risks our dogs impose, which are by far outweighed by their companionship and loyalty. After all, most things we do impose a potential health risk, even our favourite hobbies. Golf may cause injury to our backs, swimming can put us in touch with many water-borne diseases and jogging is now causing more and more joint injuries. The world would be a sorrier place without our hobbies and even sorrier without our pets.

Man has become top dog because he had the ability to adapt to his environment, obtain safe food and water and control the infections to which all animals are exposed. One of his basic needs is companionship and that of fellow human beings has not sufficed, so he has always added pets of one kind or another. Dogs have held high priority and their aptitude for training and discipline ensures that with good management any related problem areas can be controlled.

The Behaviourist's Point of View

Surely we must all express our emotions. We cuddle and kiss our children, hopefully we kiss our spouse, and we shake hands when we greet our friends. It is quite natural for dogs to gently nibble as a greeting. However this practice is considered antisocial, perhaps with the worry that this may propagate biting in the future. So we stop the nipping. *Then what?* How does our dog now show us affection? The only method now available is licking. This must surely be desirable so that a close bond is established with our dog and that he does not feel rejected. This is particularly relevant with parents of young children who often become positively neurotic when the dog approaches to show affection. The parents may shout hysterically at the dog, physically separate it from the child and then cannot understand why a bonding has not taken place between the two.

The Doctor's Point of View

"The playful puppies' nibbles

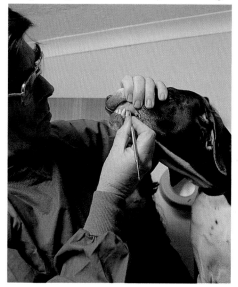

ORAL HYGIENE. Periodic check-ups by your veterinarian will alert you to any problems with your dog's mouth. Photo by R. Hutchings.

are not dangerous and are not likely to go septic as their mouth is probably far cleaner than their owners'!"

The Veterinarian's Point of View

Always assuming that your dog's mouth is cared for in the same way as you would take care of his coat by grooming, (teeth are kept clean, gums fresh and the dog is not allowed to lick other dogs' urine or eat faeces) then the veterinarian would agree with the behaviourist's point of view.

WILL MY DOG BITE/SAVAGE MY CHILD?

Perhaps the question should read "Why are parents so concerned that their dog would attack their child?"

Statistically there would be no greater chance of such an occurrence than say a wife attacking her husband with a rolling pin. It is far less likely than being mugged on the streets of London, New York or Tokyo. In essence dogs are extremely reliable, tolerant and loving although sensible precautions must always be in order, such as not leaving a young baby alone with the dog or allowing a toddler to molest your canine friend. An account springs to mind of a dog who badly bit a child. The dog was put down, but the vet, concerned at this unusual behaviour from his well-known patient, carried out a complete post-mortem only to find to his horror that the dog had a pencil

A KISS AND A CUDDLE. As long as your dog's mouth is clean and well-cared-for, a nibble or lick is just a harmless display of love and affection. Photo by R. Hutchings.

lodged in his brain by way of the ear!

Perhaps the most volatile scenario is when a young baby arrives home: the mother's protective instinct is at its peak as she holds this tiny baby, dad is also proud and protective and granny has tunnel vision. The question is who loses? The dog, of course. The family's affection is suddenly switched from the dog to the child, his interest in the new arrival is met with rebuff and his advances result in paranoid protectiveness. Imagine you are Ryder Cup captain for three years but the next competition relegates you to reserve player. How would you feel? Please, please, please, when baby arrives back home include your dog in your love and P.S. keep granny in tow!

Choosing the Breed for You

Remember, your dog should be your pal for the next ten or more years. We will examine the requirements of various purebred dogs by itemizing the following:

BREED

We have only selected the most popular international breeds for this section.

When obtaining any dog, the potential owner should be aware that within each breed differences in character, energy and fitness are normal.

If in doubt consult a specialist book on your choice of dog, talk to breeders, vets, trainers and above all, make your choice based on the *individual* dog.

HOME

We have attempted to divide breeds into two categories, those suitable for either apartment or house and those where a house and garden are essential. You may, for example, be surprised that a Newfoundland could be considered for a flat. But this choice is based on the normal, calm and placid nature of the breed and assumes that the apartment has easy access to street level. Walking up and down three flights of stairs would render your dwelling unsuitable. Imagine your Newfie has just returned from the vet still under the influence of the anaesthetic and has to be carried upstairs.

A Great Dane would surely be unsuited for life in a small mobile home, but if for some reason circumstances forced you to move from a house, it must be better for your dog's sake if it spends the rest of its years with you despite the less-than-ideal conditions. In contrast, the Miniature Poodle may be ideally suited for apartment living, but a hyper-active example of the breed may prove a headache in such an environment.

EXERCISE

Of course the level of exercise must be determined by the age and fitness of the individual dog. The period when peak fitness should be expected is from one to six years of age.

GROOMING

All dogs will need some grooming in order to maintain a healthy coat, but some will require special grooming. The Yorkshire Terrier, for example, who does not moult, will require such care and if this needs to be carried out professionally an additional expense is incurred.

Consult your canine beautician *first*.

FOOD

This category is divided into small, medium and large eaters.

Again this will depend on the dog's level of regular exercise and fitness. The Border Collie working many hours a day will require more food than one who is left during working hours and only receives a one-hour walk a day. In general, castrated dogs and spayed bitches should be encouraged to eat slightly less food. *Obesity may cause premature disease and death.*

CHILDREN

Of course the young toddler pulling a dog's tail or ears is likely to exasperate even the most placid of dogs.

The Rottweiler and American Pit Bull Terrier have in recent years caused considerable worry in the U.K. due to a few appalling attacks on children. Whilst a new owner with young children may be unwise to buy such breeds, this in no way implies that dogs of such notorious breeds, which may also include the German Shepherd Dog, Dobermann, Malamute, Staffordshire Bull Terrier, etc., do not live very happily with children and pose no threat whatsoever. It is our advice, however, to choose a breed known for its love of children and generally gentle disposition.

ELDERLY

Those who are of retirement age and over have the great gift of time to offer their dogs, which people with young families and jobs may not have. However, care must be taken in choosing your breed as over ten years or more of your dog's life you may experience great physical changes more than any other time in your life.

HEALTH

Some breeds have genetic disorders, such as the German Shepherd Dog, who is highly prone to hip dysplasia, or the Dachshund, who is more likely to have spinal disorders than other breeds. *Serious disorders may prove very expensive.*

TRAINING

In our context, training refers only to obedience training. It is

AM I THE BEST DOG FOR YOU? Is the Staffordshire Bull Terrier, for example, a good choice of dog for a household with young children? Some would say yes. Photo by M. Rolson.

perhaps a little unfair to lump all members of a particular breed as poor, fair or good but to expect a Lhasa Apso to do the heel work of a Border Collie, or a Chow Chow to do scent discrimination would be more unfair.

There will always be the exceptionally talented dog with the exceptionally talented owner who will prove to be the exception to the rule. Conversely there will always be the dog from a normally highly intelligent breed to whom nothing gets through. So this is intended as a general guide to an average of that type.

THE CROSS-BREED

These dogs will often show the tendencies of both lines. A Border Collie-German Shepherd Dog cross may, for example, have the Border's insatiable need to work and learn combined with the strong, protective instincts of the Alsatian.

THE "57" VARIETY

A definitive appraisal for mutts is tantamount to impossible and these dogs can only be judged on individual merit. Food and exercise levels will only truly be known after the dog is fully grown.

Mongrels tend to be well disposed towards children and less prone to serious genetic disorders. (Although it must be said that perhaps owners are less pre-conditioned to investigate genetic disorders.)

Remember, if you choose a mongrel you will have a unique dog—there will only be one like it in the world!

A NICE EXAMPLE OF A CROSS-BREED. This is Lucy, a ten-month-old Corgi-cross. Photo by Mrs. H.J. Wilkinson.

BREED	Home	Exercise	Grooming	Food	Children	Elderly	Health	Training
Afghan Hound								
Airedale Terrier								
Alaskan Malamute								
Anatolian Karabash								
Basset Hound								
Beagle								
Bearded Collie								
Belgian Shepherd								
Bernese Mt. Dog								
Bichon Frise								
Border Collie								
Boxer								
Briard								
Bulldog								
Bullmastiff								
Bull Terrier								
Cavalier King Charles Spaniel								
Chihuahua								
Chow Chow								
Corgis								
Dachshund								
Dalmatian								
Dobermann								
German Shepherd Dog								
Great Dane								
Greyhound								
Irish Wolfhound								
Jack Russell Terrier								

BREED	Home	Exercise	Grooming	Food	Children	Elderly	Health	Training
Lhasa Apso								
Mastiff (English)								
Maremma Sheepdog								
Newfoundland								
Old English Sheepdog								
Papillon								
Pekingese								
Pointer								
Poodle, Miniature								
Poodle, Standard								
Pug								
Pyrenean Mt. Dog								
Retrievers —all types								
Rhodesian Ridgeback								
Rottweiler								
Rough Collie								
St. Bernard								
Samoyed								
Schnauzer								
Schnauzer, Giant								
Setters—Irish, English, Gordon								
Shetland Sheepdog								
Shih Tzu								
Spaniel, Cocker								
Spaniels—Field, Irish, Water								
Spaniel, Springer								
Staffordshire Bull Terrier								

BREED	Home	Exercise	Grooming	Food	Children	Elderly	Health	Training
Terriers:								
Border	Apartment or house	Small amount	Some grooming	Small eater	Suitable*	Suitable elderly	Good health	Poor
Cairn	Apartment or house	Small amount	Special grooming	Small eater	Suitable*	Suitable elderly	Good health	Poor
Welsh	Apartment or house	Large amount	Special grooming	Small eater	Suitable*	Suitable elderly	Good health	Fair
West Highland White	Apartment or house	Small amount	Special grooming	Small eater	Suitable*	Suitable elderly*	Genetic disorders	Fair
Yorkshire	Apartment or house	Small amount	Special grooming	Small eater	Suitable*	Suitable elderly*	Genetic disorders	Poor
Weimaraner	House & garden essential	Large amount	Some grooming	Small eater	Suitable	Suitable elderly	Good health	Good
Whippet	House & garden essential	Large amount	Some grooming	Small eater	Suitable	Suitable elderly	Good health	Fair

Chart design by P. Beavis.

KEY TO SYMBOLS

- Suitable for apartment or house
- House & garden essential
- Small amount of exercise
- Large amount of exercise
- Medium amount of exercise
- Special grooming
- Some grooming
- Small eater
- Medium eater
- Large eater
- Genetic disorders
- Good health
- Poor
- Good
- Fair

*Huge individual characteristics

- Suitable for children
- Unsuitable for children
- Suitable for elderly people
- Unsuitable for elderly people

The Difficult Ages

2-4 months	Wetting and messing.
3-6 months	Teething (possibly causing chewing problems).
6 months-1 year	Puberty in male dogs with possible hormone-related problems.
6-18 months	Puberty in female dogs. First season should occur.
5 years +	Varies hugely with breed of dog and with individuals.

WHEN I GROW UP...This five-year-old Bichon-Lhasa-cross had to go through the difficult ages before becoming this well mannered (and well dressed!). Photo by D. Allen.

Acquiring Your Dog

If you are a novice at buying dogs, a professional trainer, an experienced club trainer or a fellow breeder will feel flattered at being asked to choose your pup with you so don't hesitate to ask. He will have a much better idea of the points to look out for. If, however, this facility is not available, then it's all up to you to make a careful selection.

In the USA a pet shop may be the most obvious place to acquire your pet dog. However, if you are seeking a show- or breeder-quality puppy or are having trouble finding your chosen breed of dog, a reputable breeder would be your best bet.

THE BREEDER

Once you have located a breeder, make an appointment to look at the litter. On arriving at the breeder's, make note of the surroundings. A well-cared-for home will probably mean that the pups have been equally well cared for. Look at the breeder's sign and note if they are specialising in your particular breed. If they have a wide variety of breeds, it may be that they are a puppy broker buying dogs of unknown origin.

Driving down the path, an onslaught of dogs barking and growling at you should be treated as a warning of the nature of the puppy you may be buying; their lack of control maybe an indication of the breeder's lax approach.

A cross-examination by the breeder about you and your circumstances should indicate to you their caring attitude towards the pups, so do not feel intimidated—the bark is probably worse than the bite.

The pups should be in a clean and warm environment, and still be with mum. If mum is not around, you should ask why as it is likely in such circumstances that the pups were not reared at this establishment. Mum should still be feeding or suckling the pups (up to six weeks) and her chest should appear sore and baggy. Even with pups of an older age, say 12 weeks, the mother will still clearly show signs of having had a recent litter. Puppies who have had a good relationship with their mother and litter mates are far less likely to have behavioural problems in their later lives. *Beware* of the puppy who has been rejected by its mother prematurely or one who has a poor relationship with its litter mates. These dogs often prove a problem as they grow older.

Most people seem tempted to buy the puppy who rushes to them. This will indicate a highly extroverted nature and is probably not the ideal choice for the inexperienced owner. Furthermore the dog who is cringing in the corner also may be considered unsuitable as it will almost certainly demonstrate nervous characteristics

IN SAFE HANDS. If a breeder asks you many questions, don't be insulted. This means that he cares about placing his puppies in a proper home. Photo by J. Combe.

MUM'S THE WORD. When you go to the breeder to visit the pups, the mother should be present. Photo by J. Combe.

SEVENTH HEAVEN. Bringing your new puppy home is an exciting time for both you and your pup. Make sure that you have everything that is needed to make your puppy feel right at home. Photo by C.R. Davis.

throughout adulthood.

If possible, try dropping a suitably noisy object such as a tin tray. The dog who jumps out of his skin will probably be of a nervous disposition and the puppy who takes no notice at all may demonstrate a hearing deficiency. We would expect the dog at four weeks plus of age to look around inquisitively but show no fright. So the ideal choice for the novice owner should be the nice, alert, middle-of-the-road puppy.

Feeding should have been carried out by the breeder using separated feeding bowls. The dog who has had to parry for his food may display more protectiveness towards his food than the dog fed separately and is more likely to bolt his food, a trait almost impossible to correct in later life. Finally having satisfied yourself in a calm and detached way, because after all most people's hearts melt at the sight of a puppy, the transaction may begin. Before making any payments ask to see the pedigree papers of both parents and any registration documents, such as the Kennel Club/American Kennel Club litter registration documents. Over a cup of tea, formalities may be sorted out and a date for picking up your puppy, probably when it is about eight weeks old, will be decided upon. You can now go home and look forward to your puppy entering your life.

CHOOSING YOUR RESCUE DOG

Thank goodness for the wonderful work that the rescue organisations perform, for without them there would be no help for the abandoned or unwanted dog.

There can be nothing more satisfying or fulfilling than happily re-housing a hitherto unwanted dog, but some degree of caution should be observed.

It is of paramount importance that a totally honest report on the dog's previous history is given to you by the representative of the rescue organisation. Sometimes, of course, such history is not available but on occasions, through the kindness of their heart, details are omitted in order that the dog be re-homed. Should the dog have been brought to them because of serious behavioural problems, rather than dismissing the dog as unsuitable, contact your behaviourist or trainer to see whether such problems can be sorted out. Aggression towards other dogs should be evident on your visit to the kennels; aggression towards humans will be even more evident. If you are planning to have your dog in a family environment, take the *whole* family along, particularly children, to ensure compatibility.

Check also the dog's medical history if available as a serious condition may prove very expensive and a history of a chronic complaint may render the dog uninsurable.

Having decided on your new partner, the rescue organisation will probably require a lot of form filling and a contribution towards their funds. Many of the organisations are as fussy about the dog's new owners as a good breeder may be, and rightly so for they do not wish to see another unhappy phase in the dog's life. Often such organisations will make a visit to determine the suitability of your home and some

A CRY FOR HELP OR A POTENTIAL PROBLEM? When rescuing a dog you should inquire about the dog's history, including any behavioural problems. Photo by T.B. Chadwick.

may back this up with subsequent calls to ensure all is well. Do not take offence as they are only looking after your dog's welfare. It is quite often the case that full legal ownership of your dog is withheld and remains in the hands of the welfare organisation. This is to ensure that, should the dog's new owners be found to be unsuitable, the dog may be taken back at any time. This does not, however, mean that items such as veterinary bills will be paid by them or that the dog is any less yours.

SEVEN THINGS TO BUY BEFORE YOU BRING YOUR PUPPY HOME

1) Dog basket or similar bedding facilities
2) Warm washable bedding, blankets, etc.
3) Feeding and water bowls
4) Puppy food
5) Safe and effective chew products (Nylabone®, Gumabone®)
6) Hot water bottle
7) Old-fashioned alarm clock that ticks

WHERE TO BUY IN THE U.K. & AUSTRALIA

In the U.K. most people will buy a pedigree dog directly from a breeder. Due to inadequate government legislation, conditions in which dogs were kept in U.K. pet shops caused such public concern that the sale of dogs through this source has largely been phased out, although some still remain maintaining much higher standards, notably Harrods department store, London, where it is claimed even an elephant can be obtained! It is also geographically easier for the potential owner to travel these relatively small distances to

CARRY ON COCKERS. The mum of the litter can tell you much about the temperament and physical type of the pups. These Cocker pups were bred by Louise Shattuck of Massachusetts.

ONE OF A KIND. Although these Springer puppies appear to be nearly identical, they each develop their own personalities, including their likes and dislikes. Your breeder can tell you much about the personality of each member of his litter.

choose their new puppy. In Australia, where distances can be a problem for the potential purchaser, the sale of dogs is still, however, mainly directly from the breeder. Legislation requires that the owners of pet shops must be resident on the premises if they are to keep animals for sale, and this has largely made this trade unattractive.

Don't rush. Buy carefully and you'll be happy with your new pup for a long time.

Bringing Your Dog Home

THE FIRST DAY—PUPPIES

The exciting day has arrived when your puppy is ready to be brought home. Remember—the day you wake up excited by the thought of your new arrival, he is sleeping content and satisfied with his mother and litter mates. To him the day will be traumatic, not exciting. Make sure you leave home adequately kitted up. Take a nice warm blanket for him to sleep in and be sure the car upholstery is protected as it is likely your young pup may have accidents on the way home. When you reach the breeder, try to spend a couple of hours with pup first, allowing him time to get to know you or even better, if the journey is not too long, how about a few familiarisation visits before the day arrives to take him home. Try to avoid travelling on a very hot day as this will cause your pup considerable stress. If necessary, travel in the cool of the evening. Don't forget, your pup will need water for the journey. Do not travel alone as the pup will certainly need comfort and restraining both for his security and yours.

When you get your puppy home he will probably be a little frightened by his new surroundings. Try not to let the family overwhelm him. Don't allow the children to rush towards him and scare him, rather they should sit patiently and await pup to approach them.

If you already have a dog, please don't forget to make at least as much fuss as normal of him, if not more. Remember, a dog whose nose is out of joint is likely to become a cross dog! Respect his position as senior dog.

At night your puppy will feel confused and very lonely, for up until now he has had the company, the warmth and the security of his fellow puppies and mum. In order to ensure the best possible chances of an uninterrupted night, make sure the pup is well tucked up with a comfortably warm hot-water bottle and an old-fashioned alarm clock beside him, the warmth and ticking sound simulating litter conditions. Snuggling up with an older dog will certainly comfort your puppy but this should not be undertaken on the first night as the dogs must be familiarised with each other until the owner is certain that the dogs are compatible.

Remember that the ground rules are set as early as the first day home. If, for example, you allow your new pup to sleep in the bedroom with you from day one, then transition to another room becomes difficult. If you rush to the dog's side when it starts to cry at night, you will similarly encourage future problems. This is hard but necessary if you insist on isolated sleeping arrangements for your dog.

NOW I'M YOURS. Training should begin from the first day you bring your puppy home. So who's going to be the boss? Photo by K. Wilkinson.

Don't forget to cover the floor with newspaper! Have a nice sleep then enjoy the first full day with your new pal.

THE FIRST DAY—RESCUE DOG

In most respects the guidelines laid down for bringing your rescue dog home are similar to those of the puppy. However expect your new dog to be heavily traumatized, suddenly coming from a kennel with many dogs around him and little human contact, into a home with possibly no other dogs and an abundance of humans, all wanting to make a fuss. Be restrained and allow him to have a good sniff around, familiarising himself with his new surroundings and making the first move to come towards the individuals in the family for attention.

A dog who feels insecure will respond far better to kind firmness than to overindulgence in affection and sentimentality, as from the moment he arrives home the ground rules will be laid.

So often we find that, through pity, owners will avoid using a firm approach, misguidedly thinking that this will result in a confident dog. However, a positive approach needs to be adopted to give the dog trust in his new pack environment.

A HOME AT LAST! Allow your new rescue dog time to become familiar with his surroundings. Photo by Z. Skivington.

THE SECOND DAY AND BEYOND

There has been much written by such eminent zoologists as Professor Konrad Lorenz and Dr. Desmond Morris about the influence of the early months in establishing the dog's future behaviour and character.

We have tried to point out ideal conditions that will foster good character. Now the ball is in your court and it is essential to familiarise and socialise your puppy correctly with the outside world. Although your puppy will not be allowed to walk around the streets until his inoculations are complete, it is worthwhile starting interaction with people and other dogs straight away on a limited basis, but not an overwhelming one. If you have friends with nice gentle (vaccinated) dogs or with children of even disposition,

SHARE AND SHARE ALIKE. Proper early socialisation is important when shaping the future character and behaviour of your dog. These two pups are learning to share with Nylafloss®. Photo by K. Taylor.

invite them to your home in order that you maximise your dog's early socialisation programme. Lack of such socialisation has proved to exacerbate problems during later development. Dogs, for example, who have not been brought up with children will prove far less tolerant towards them than those who have always been exposed to such company. The one-dog-litter syndrome often puts such a dog at a great disadvantage when interacting with other dogs later in life.

Remember dogs do not like to be "rushed at" so let the dog come to you or your children.

Be sure from this day that you are able to take food and toys from your dog without him showing aggression. Remember your dog is going to get a lot bigger and any problems will get bigger too!

SOME MAJOR NO-NOS!

1) Do not use rolled-up newspapers to chastise your dog. Later in life he may start attacking them or people carrying them.

2) For the same reason, do not use a stick.

3) Do not rub your dog's nose in his mess. It will teach him nothing and will certainly confuse him.

4) Do not feed your pup from the table, as it will become a lifelong habit.

5) Do not leave your puppy for long periods of time.

6) A playful pup is not a naughty pup. Be firm but allow him his youthful joy for life.

Caring for Your New Companion

FEEDING YOUR PUPPY

Now that you have brought your puppy home, one of the first considerations is how to feed him. In most cases the breeder will have given you a diet sheet or will have told you of the diet that it has been fed. If this information is not supplied, do ask. It is best to try and follow this diet as closely as you can for the first few days. Changing homes will have been a very stressful experience for your puppy so it is better not to add to the stress by changing his diet; it is more reassuring to have familiar food when faced with a new and strange world. After the first few days you can gradually introduce the diet of your choice.

Usually eight-week-old puppies are fed four times a day. If you choose a good manufactured puppy food, this will contain all the nutrients needed. Additional vitamin and mineral supplements need not be fed.

As a general guide, if your puppy has not eaten all the food after twenty minutes, the remainder should be removed and, if perishable, thrown away. However, should your puppy refuse food on repeated occasions, consult your veterinarian.

Your puppy may already be on a diet that is composed of fresh ingredients such as meat, cereal, eggs and milk. Usually two meat-based meals and two milk-based meals daily may be suggested. Eggs should be fed cooked because raw eggs can prevent the proper assimilation of essential vitamins. As a puppy grows, quantities should be increased. Generally at 12 to 16 weeks old, puppies can receive only three daily meals. Sometimes your puppy will start refusing part or all of one of the daily meals, usually one of the milk meals. This is an excellent guide for you to cut down to one milk and two regular meals.

Some dogs cannot digest the lactose in ordinary cow's milk and feeding it may cause diarrhoea. In this case try feeding a proprietary dog's milk substitute or cut the milk out altogether.

Home assembled diets *must* include a balanced mineral and vitamin supplement. These are readily available from your pet shop or veterinary surgery and will include instructions.

Diarrhoea is probably the most common digestive problem faced by owners. If diarrhoea is violent or persists for more than 24 hours see your veterinarian, after all your puppy is only a baby and should not be allowed to become seriously ill before you seek professional help.

EXPERT GUIDE ON NUTRITION
by Göran Heyman

A long time ago the dog was mainly used as a helper by humans for hunting, guarding, pulling, etc. Nowadays the dog is considered to be an important member of the family, a member of the family who becomes more humanised and is considered as a child. This is noticeable in the modern language, more often we hear such words as giving the dog his "dinner" instead of his "feed".

How should you feed your dog? How much should we consider the dog and how much should we consider his master and mistress? Obviously it is the dog's needs that are most important many people would say, but is this the case? For the dog the choice of food is according to the smell. Smell will be its prime sense when selecting food although this may not always be as appealing to his master and mistress. This is noticeable when the food is kept in a larder. The manufacturers of dog food must take this into consideration and compromise between the human and the animal requirements. How weird, says the dog food manufacturer, our customers are six-legged!

Different types of dog food

There are three main types of dog food: dry food, canned food and semi-produce (which is a cross between tin food and dry food). All these products consist of the same base products but are

FOLLOW YOUR NOSE...For a dog, smell is the number one factor when selecting food, although his owners might not agree. Photo by I. Francais.

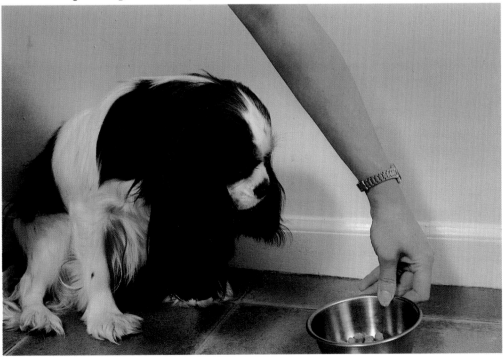

developed in different ways.

In *dry dog food* the water has been removed from the base product in such a way that 10% of the water is left. This means that the food can be stored in an opened bag at room temperature without being damaged. It is also common practice to add water to the food before it is served to the dog, which means that the extracted water is now put back again.

There are various production techniques:

1) Extruding is the most common method for dry food. In principle this is fast pressure cooking under high temperature. Thereafter the product is dried.

2) Baking is the most common method in the U.K. In the rough dough, baking powders are mixed in and the product is baked in large ovens where it rises and dries.

The ingredients are mixed after they have been cooked, dried, baked or puffed up. Quite often vegetables are added in order to make it more appealing to the owner.

3) The third type of dry dog food consists of various mixers. The raw materials are first ground and mixed, thereafter extruded or baked. Mixers consist of a concoction of ready baked, puffed up, extruded or untreated products that are mixed at the final stage.

Canned food is preserved dog food with a water content of 75–80%. This is the natural water content, which is mainly included in meat products. In order to make the product storable at room temperature it is sterilised and thereafter put in an airtight container that is usually made of tin but can also be made of plastic and aluminum. The most apparent difference between dry food and canned food is usually that the dry food is much cheaper but the canned food tastes better. If the water is extracted the canned food contains more protein and fat than dry food.

Semi-produce foods come in different types, which consist of parts of dry food and meat products mixed, with a water content of 18–20%. In order for these products to be stored at room temperature, various preservatives are added.

What does the dog want to eat?

What does the dog like to eat best? Well, what the other members of the family are eating right now for dinner. One way to solve this problem, and at the same time be kind to the wallet, is to let the dog get used to a complete dry food and then add scraps from the dinner table, which the dog has already enjoyed smelling during the family meal. The dog should always have his meal last and should, strictly speaking, not be allowed to sit and beg at the dinner table.

Is it wrong to only give leftovers to your dog?

This depends upon what is left over on the plate. Rich gravy, chips and an odd biscuit don't make a dog healthy. Instead, giving the dog

A DOG'S DINNER. Unlike us humans, a varied diet is unnecessary for dogs. Too many changes may cause upset tummies. Photo by I. Francais.

a little bit of what you have just eaten with the complete dry food of your choice added would give the best results. As a general rule, dogs don't need to have a varied diet. It is only we human beings that feel like changing it. Humans cause more trouble by mixing a lot of different things together in a dog's diet. It is more difficult for the naturally occurring bacteria in the intestine of the dog to adjust to different types of food in comparison with the human. It is because of this that there are so many different tastes of the same type of food—a varied diet without changing the basic ingredients.

Different Dogs, Different Foods

Do different breeds have different dietary needs with the exception of how much they eat? In principle the same type of food can be used for all types of dogs. What can vary is each individual dog's situation. There are special diets for puppies, old dogs, working dogs, unwell dogs, over-weight dogs, etc. Independent of what breed they are, small dogs often eat preserved food whilst large dogs usually eat complete dry food. This is something of a fallacy invented by humans. If dry food is given at the puppy stage, it is imprinted upon the dog for life. If one wants the dog to eat dry food as an older dog, it is easier if this food is given from puppyhood.

Quality Commercial Foods

On the side of the packaging one can read the different ingredients used for a particular food. It could be meat and meat derivatives, fish, chicken, cereal and often minerals and vitamins, in principle the same raw materials as we are eating. The difference is that dog food uses various off-cuts that cannot be used for human consumption. The raw materials are mixed to a particular recipe in the same way as we prepare our dinner at home. In order to make sure that the food has the correct nutritional value, regular checks are carried out on the raw materials as well as the ready-made food. In this instance one can also check the correct levels of protein, fat, carbohydrates, minerals and vitamins.

Why is this so important? We don't even check our own food that carefully; we simply vary different types of food during different meals. Dry food is put together in such a way that one diet should cover the dog's complete needs.

It is essential that kenneled dogs, such as police or army dogs, receive a diet that completely fulfills their needs, as they do not receive titbits or extras in the same way as most family dogs.

How much food shall I give to my dog?

It is important not to follow the recommended quantities too literally. Dogs are exactly the same as we human beings, some are slightly over-weight whilst others can eat as much as they like without putting on weight. Another important factor is how

SOMEONE'S BEEN EATING MY PORRIDGE...Puppies and adult dogs have different dietary needs. Make sure you follow the feeding guidelines on the packaging of your chosen dog food. Photo by I. Francais.

active the dog is. The feeding chart on the packaging should only be used as a guideline. The most important thing is that you regularly look after your dog and make sure that your dog is not over- or under-weight. It should be noted that the dog's needs are in relation to his correct surface area, not his weight.

How does one know that the dog food is a complete dog food?

There has been world-wide study regarding the dog's nutritional needs. The generally accepted research is that of the National Research Council (N.R.C.).

The main dog food manufacturers are very much in accord with the N.R.C. when producing their own brand. Currently within Europe there is collaboration between the manufacturers and the E.E.C. Commission in Brussels to create quality and standardised guidelines for food.

Not all dog food is in the form of a complete diet. Certain products must be mixed with different types of ingredients to produce a diet that covers the dog's nutritional needs. These products are called food supplements and feeding instructions must be printed on the packaging to this effect.

How is the dog food tested?

Before a new dog food product is launched on the market it has been carefully tested by the manufacturer over a long period of time. Tests are carried out where a number of dogs are only fed on this type of food and water over a six month period, being closely monitored by a veterinarian.

A canine taste panel is created with a number of dogs that are given the choice as to which food they prefer. In addition, marketing tests are completed where the owners can air their opinion about the packaging, smell, etc.

Can all dogs tolerate all dog foods?

Dogs are all individuals, as are human beings.

Nowadays allergies are more and more common amongst dogs. A small percentage of these are caused by diet as with humans who are allergic to, for example, tomatoes or shellfish. There are dogs that are allergic to a certain raw material in a particular food. It is important to understand that it is not the fault of the manufacturer but a problem for the dog that has a weakness for a certain raw material. It can be difficult to find out to which substance the dog is allergic. Over long periods of time selected types of basic food should be systematically tested as has been written by our doctor citing the Great Ormond Street studies on children. If you have success in finding to which basic ingredient, or ingredients, your dog is allergic, it is best to avoid these in the future (as with humans).

What does futuristic dog food look like?

The dog's future diet (equally the human diet) is completely dependent upon the resources of raw materials available on the Earth. Try to imagine that six million dogs eat on average 300g. of food per day, this means 1,800 tonnes per day, or approximately 100 container loads per day. This would give an idea of the dimensions involved concerning all dogs on Earth.

It is important that we as dog owners do not compete with the human food consumption in a world where the basic food availability gets less and less. It is up to the manufacturer to preserve and treat the food with suitable processes so that the nutritional value and taste maintain the highest standards. All this so that human's best friend—the dog—shall be fit and well without unnecessary consumption of human food.

VACCINATIONS (MAKING A POINT!)

It is vital that you have your puppy vaccinated against the most important infectious diseases of dogs. These diseases frequently kill dogs; at best they damage your puppy's health.

Puppies are normally vaccinated to prevent their contracting distemper, parvovirus and some liver and kidney infections caused by viruses and bacteria. Your puppy can also be vaccinated against kennel cough

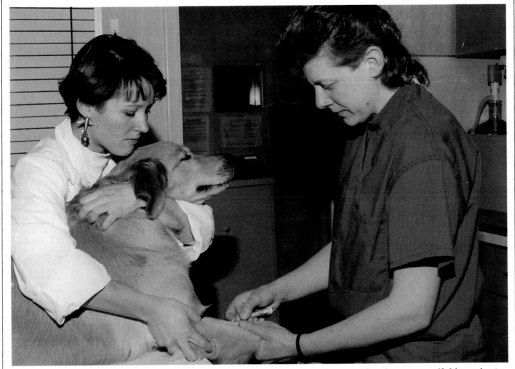

HOLD ME CLOSE, MUM. It is always best to take your dog to the veterinarian yourself. Your doctor may ask questions that only you will know. Photo by K. Taylor.

which, although usually cured easily, is an infectious cough that is most distressing to your dog and may last several weeks.

The vaccinations can start when your puppy is six weeks old, although sometimes they are given as late as eight to 12 weeks; and often a third vaccination at 16 weeks is recommended. Your veterinarian will know the current disease situation in your area and will be happy to advise you of the best course of vaccination for your puppy. It is sensible to keep your puppy away from possible sources of infections, such as public areas, until after the 12-week vaccination, although early socialisation with other dogs is

equally desirable in order to ensure their future behavioural patterns. Therefore a compromise solution, such as inviting friends with their fully vaccinated dogs to your house for early interaction, is suggested.

Dogs need booster vaccinations annually.

CHEWING OVER THE PROBLEMS OF TEETHING

Probably one of the most traumatic experiences that your puppy will go through in its life is that of teething.

As your puppy was probably not brought home until the age of six weeks or more, he will already have a full set of milk teeth. These closely resemble needles which can be a painful experience for the owner who will probably be subjected to the puppy's nibbling on their hands for relief and comfort.

Your puppy should be discouraged from this nipping by reasonably firm reprimand but another chewing item must be given to him, such as a Nylabone®, in order that he can massage his gums and exercise his jaws in the way nature intended. Old shoes or slippers are not a good idea; in later life it may become your new shoes or slippers that your dog chews. At the age of 12 weeks or thereabouts, however, your pup will start to cut his adult or permanent teeth.

This can be an extremely uncomfortable period and it is important to understand that acts of chewing on furniture, carpets or even parts of the human anatomy in no way reflect a behavioural problem. It is simply your dog's method of relieving pain. Of course it must be stressed that such behaviour, if allowed to continue after teething, may lead to continued undesirable behaviour in later life.

It would be considered improper in this instance to use a high level of compulsion, smacking your puppy, as the dog's desire level, the pain, is so high that a sufficient level would be considered unkind and in any case simply would not work.

We therefore redress our scales by reducing the desire level. This being done by means of painkillers, which can be obtained from your veterinarian or proprietary children's analgesics (ideally agreed to by your vet), in addition gum treatments used for children can equally be used on your dog's gums.

Should the nipping/biting become excessive, a tap on the jowls as the dog's head comes forward is acceptable accompanied by a command such as "No bites." On cessation your dog, as always, should be praised (even if you feel he should not have done it in the first place).

Serious puppy biting may require you to push your dog's jowls in, thus causing him to bite himself, making him cognisant of his own actions.

Teaching a puppy takes time and he will undoubtedly try over and over again until the message sinks in and/or the pain has abated, but rest assured that sooner rather than later this problem will be a thing of the past.

Occasionally a puppy/dog may develop an abscess so, if chewing reaches unacceptably excessive limits, consult your veterinarian who will check out your dog's mouth.

It is important to understand, during this period of bringing up your puppy, that the owner is at home almost all of the day in order to divert and stimulate the puppy in the correct way. It is very easy to stop a puppy chewing your best shoes by substituting a chew-stick or

TEETHING. During the time that your puppy begins to cut his adult teeth, it is a good idea to give him a safe chew toy, such as a Nylabone®, to massage his gums. Jacquet Boxer pup bred by Richard Tomita. Photo by I. Francais.

Nylabone® if you are present, but impossible if you are not.

Note: The Next Few Paragraphs Are Not Suitable For After-Dinner Conversation!

"WORMINOLOGY"—YOUR PUPPY AND WORMS

The thought that your puppy will have worms is unpleasant; however, these revolting things are unbelievably successful parasites. The two main types are **roundworms** (Nematodes) and **tapeworms** (Cestodes). Roundworms include hookworms, toxocara species, and whipworms. A brief description of their life cycles will help you understand how to control them. Adult roundworms, of which the most important is *Toxocara canis (T.canis)*, look rather like pieces of spaghetti. They are whitish in colour, generally about 4-10 centimetres long and have pointed ends. They may be seen in the faeces or, in heavier infestations, may be produced in vomit. The adult worms live in the intestine where the female worm lays large numbers of eggs that then pass out in the faeces. After a maturation period on the ground, the eggs become infective and if swallowed by the dog, the larvae hatch out of the eggs, migrate through the body and eventually return to the intestine to develop into adult worms. In adult dogs many of the larvae do not return to the intestines; they become dormant in the body tissues. When a bitch is pregnant these dormant stages can mobilise and are able to migrate into the womb to infect the unborn puppies. It is most likely that your puppy will have roundworms when you buy it, in spite of the best endeavours of the breeder. There is now available a new treatment regimen that can reduce the transmission of toxocara infection from the bitch and her pups by 98%, though it would still be necessary in some cases to treat the pups before they leave the kennels as they can also pick up toxocara infection in the kennels and runs. Repeated treatment of puppies may be necessary as not all wormers are effective against larval stages.

It is also very important to pick up and dispose of your puppy's faeces as soon as possible thus reducing the number of eggs contaminating the environment and the level of challenge to your puppy.

The main groups of tapeworms are *Dipylidium caninum, Taenia* species and the tiny *Echinococcus granulosus*. They have a head that is attached to the wall of the intestine and a segmented body. Segments containing the eggs are passed in the faeces; sometimes they wriggle out of the anus and become attached to the dog's coat where they may look like a dried up grain of rice. To complete the life cycle, the eggs must pass through another host, such as a rodent, sheep or, most commonly, the flea. Your dog becomes infected by eating this intermediate host. Therefore tapeworms are more likely to be a problem in the older puppy or adult dog. Tapeworms are relatively easy to eliminate using an appropriate remedy, again your vet can advise you. It is important to follow the directions of the particular remedy carefully, and to control the intermediate hosts, particularly fleas, so that re-infection can be prevented.

Worms are such successful parasites that you must treat puppies and adult dogs regularly to prevent heavy infestations. It is generally recommended that adult dogs are treated every three to six months.

Hookworms are small thin roundworms, about 12 millimetres long. There are two main genera, *Uncinaria* (otherwise known as the northern hookworm) and the *Ancylostoma* (otherwise known as the tropical hookworm).

In the U.K. and Eire the *Uncinaria* infection occurs usually in kenneled dogs, such as Greyhounds and Foxhounds, being prevalent in Eire. Heavy infections cause diarrhoea, tiredness and loss of appetite. This causes the dog to lose weight and in young dogs may slow the rate of growth. The tropical hookworm, *Ancylostoma*, which may be found in imported dogs, feeds on blood. In some countries they can be a major problem. The larvae enter the dog's body by the mouth or they can also penetrate the skin, usually the feet, where they may cause lesions. In addition puppies may become infected by way of mother's milk. The adult worms in the intestine feed on blood, with heavy infestations, causing digestive upsets and anaemia. Diagnosis of both types of hookworm is usually made by laboratory examination of the faeces for eggs.

Whipworms are another small roundworm that bury their heads in the lining of the intestine.

Infections often do not produce

FAST AND FIT. Although this Greyhound is healthy, Greyhounds kenneled for racing are prone to *Uncinaria* infection, a type of hookworm. Photo by M. Eastwood.

any illness, although your dog may lose weight and have intermittent diarrhoea. Hookworm and whipworm infections can be difficult to diagnose clinically. They can be difficult to eliminate from kennels particularly those with grass runs. The eggs can remain dormant in the ground for very long periods of time so that your dog is easily re-infected. It is best to consult your veterinarian for treatment.

LET'S ERADICATE THE LITTLE BLIGHTERS FOREVER

There are two main lines of attack. The first is to free dogs from infection and kill off, not just the adult worms, but also the larvae of toxocara that lie dormant in the female waiting to invade her pups. The life cycle of the parasite has been clearly defined with its vulnerable moments and the weapons are available. Thanks to new developments by the pharmaceutical companies treating the expectant mother at the right time of her pregnancy, the puppies after birth and adult dogs at regular intervals could ultimately eliminate this threat. Even if the bitch has been treated effectively during the last one-third of her pregnancy, the pups will probably require at least one treatment before leaving the kennels as they can pick up infection from the kennels and runs.

Meanwhile there is a great deal that can be done to cut down the existing danger and this is the big challenge for everyone who owns a dog—a mental label attached to the tail saying "what passes by here is *my* responsibility".

FLEAS—SCRATCHING FOR ANSWERS!

Constant scratching is usually the first indication that your puppy may have fleas. If you examine the skin carefully, particularly along the back and the root of the tail, you may find fleas moving through the coat or small, black "flea dirt", which is fleas' faeces containing dried blood. If you add water to flea dirt it turns red. The adult female flea lays many eggs that can drop from your puppy onto the bed, carpet and other household furnishings. The immature stages of the flea can survive for many months before reinfesting your dog, therefore regular treatment of your pet is necessary to control the production of eggs. This is particularly important during warm weather when fleas are at their most active. Bathing in an insecticidal shampoo will kill all the fleas on your dog, even if he is heavily infected. However this will not prevent him from becoming infected with new fleas from the environment. You should treat him at weekly or fortnightly intervals with insecticidal powder or sprays. Alternatively, he can wear a collar which has been impregnated with an insecticide. However, on occasion, dogs can be allergic to these collars. Hair loss from the neck area may indicate this, so of course you must remove the collar.

DON'T HANG AROUND ME. Fleas are most active in the warmer weather. Make sure that your dog is well protected by a flea collar, spray or powder during these seasons. Photo by T.B. Chadwick.

FLEE FREE. Your vet can treat your dog with an insecticide that will keep him flea-free for up to a month. Photo by R. Hutchings.

The most recent treatment available from your veterinarian is an insecticide that is absorbed through your dog's skin. A few drops placed on the skin between the shoulder blades should keep your dog free from fleas for a month.

WARNING: Insecticides are poisonous. Do not use more than one kind of treatment on your dog at any one time. Most importantly, keep all flea treatments, including collars, out of the reach of children.

Normal household cleaning with regular use of a vacuum cleaner having a flea collar in the bag is usually sufficient to control fleas in the house. However, if a heavy infestation problem does arise, your pet shop and veterinary surgeon will have products available to treat the furnishings.

Remember to use furnishing products on the furniture and dog products on the dog! Fleas bite not only dogs but also their owners, although curiously they more frequently bite the lady of the house than the man. There does not seem to be any good explanation for this—unless fleas are feminists!

KENNEL COUGH

Kennel cough is a highly contagious cough, which is very distressing to both the dog and owner. The dog suffers from continual, loud and uncontrollable coughing, which can go on day and night. Although reasonably easy to cure, the cough can persist for weeks. Your veterinarian will treat it with antibiotics and, where necessary,

HOP OFF! Products to treat household furnishings infested with fleas are available from your vet and pet shop. Photo by R. Hutchings.

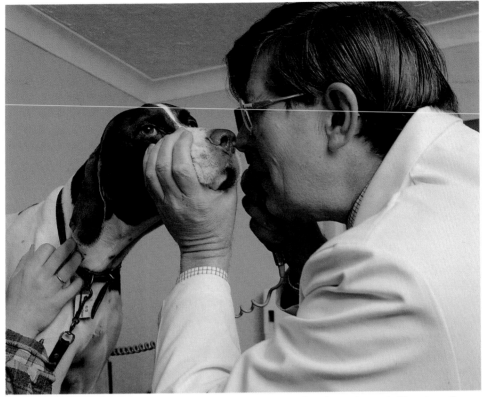

FACE TO FACE. Currently there are effective vaccines against kennel cough. However, if your dog suffers from this infection, seek treatment from your vet. Photo by R. Hutchings.

take steps to relieve the cough.

The cause of the infection is complicated. It is a mixed infection of a bacterium and a virus. Antibiotics can be used to kill the bacterium, but are not effective against the virus. The dog's own immune system has to cope with this.

As the name implies, kennel cough is often contracted when your dog is in kennels where there is a large mixed population of dogs. This is not a fault of the kennel management. It is simply a situation similar to a large number of school children catching "flu" from each other. Also, it is easily contracted from any dog that is carrying the organisms. There are now effective vaccines against kennel cough and many boarding establishments ask that your dog should be vaccinated. This can be done at the same time as the annual vaccination for distemper. Your veterinarian will recommend the best vaccination course for your dog.

Neutering

There is a major practical reason for neutering dogs (the obvious one): to prevent them from breeding and producing unwanted puppies. If you allow this to happen, somebody will have the distressing and thankless task of killing those puppies. In recent years there have been vigorous campaigns in the U.K. and the U.S.A. encouraging people to have their dogs neutered to prevent them from breeding. However, the number of unwanted dogs destroyed each year continues to rise. Why?

It seems likely that it is the responsible owners who are least likely to allow uncontrolled breeding of their dogs; they are the people most likely to listen to the advice given and have their dogs neutered. The irresponsible owner is much less likely either to listen to this advice, go to the expense of having their dog neutered or to prevent their dogs from breeding. It is the irresponsible owners and the unscrupulous, who breed dogs for purely commercial reasons, who allow unplanned and uncontrolled breeding by their dogs with no consideration to the welfare of their dogs and their puppies. Such irresponsibility accounts for the hundreds of thousands of dogs that have to be destroyed every year.

So what should you do regarding neutering your own newly acquired pet? If you are not able to prevent your dog, whether male or female, from potentially breeding, then you should consider neutering. However, neutering dogs has undesirable effects on your dog's health and these are covered in some depth later in this section. This is something you should consider when you decide to buy a dog. Should you have a dog at all if you will have difficulty keeping it under control?

If you want a dog to guard your home, neutering may remove most of the dog's guarding instincts. It is pointless to buy such a dog and then have him neutered because you cannot control him. It is much better to buy a dog that you can control in the first place.

However, if your dog is not neutered, there are hormone-related diseases to which it will remain susceptible. In later life the male dog may suffer from enlargement of or (much more rarely) cancer of the prostate gland. The bitch that is not neutered is more likely to develop tumors of the breast, which are sometimes cancerous, as she gets older. She may need a hysterectomy because of a disease of the womb called pyometra.

Many dogs are neutered to solve problems with their social or sexual behaviour. However,

A STITCH IN TIME. Many dogs are destroyed each year due to the irresponsibility of owners who allow uncontrolled and unplanned breeding. Photo by T.B. Chadwick.

many of these problems can be cured in other ways. Dogs, like people, were made male and female. Removing their sex, by castrating male dogs or spaying bitches, is a major surgical mutilation and should only be undertaken when absolutely necessary since it deprives them of all, or nearly all, of their sex hormones.

The lack of these hormones can affect the way other parts of the body work. The most obvious change is that many neutered dogs put on an excessive amount of weight and it is extremely difficult or impossible to control this excess weight by diet. Think very carefully before having your dog neutered; there usually is a better way to solve the problem.

THE MALE DOG

If you have a problem with your male dog arising from his sexuality it will fall into one of two categories.

He may show excessive and, to us, undesirable sexual behaviour or he may become aggressive, and seek to become dominant. Of course the same dog may show both types of conduct. It is perfectly natural that your dog will show an interest in bitches, even when they are not in season. While this may cause social difficulties for you it should not be a serious problem. Excessive sexual behaviour will vary from fanatical marking of territory, which may occur indoors, to mounting available objects and, more embarrassingly, people. Aggression may arise from a

desire to guard his territory or, more seriously, a desire to dominate you. Your dog may defy you and may react aggressively to commands that he previously obeyed.

Your dog's excessive sexual behaviour or aggression may arise at puberty or may arise from the desire to exert his dominance in the household when there is a change in circumstances, such as the introduction of other dogs. These problems may only be temporary, but obviously they need to be sorted out. However, most of the time, they can be put right without resorting to the extreme measure of castrating your dog.

Your veterinarian may be able to help with advice and can prescribe hormone treatment, such as Megestrol Acetate, which will decrease your dog's sexuality. You should regard this kind of treatment as a temporary measure and use the opportunity to regain control of your dog. With a difficult dog you should seek the help of your professional trainer/ behaviourist. Ask him and your veterinarian to work together to correct your problem dog.

You may need to use this drug for a few weeks until behavioural modification has been established; occasionally, however, some dogs need treatment with a low level (maintenance) dose for a longer time.

Nelson is a very large Labrador who is now four years old. When he was about a year old almost

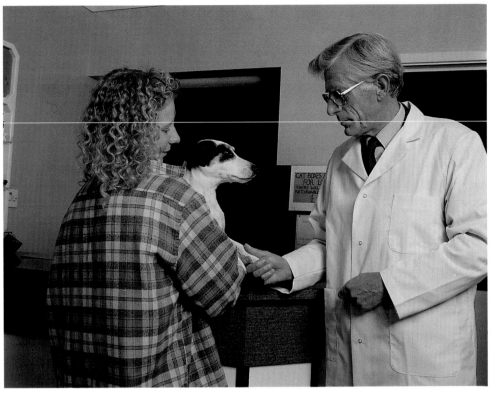

SEX QUESTIONS TO ASK YOUR VET. Other options besides neutering are available for controlling your dog's sexual behaviour. Consult your vet to find out the best treatment for your dog. Photo by R. Hutchings.

anything would create uncontrollable and embarrassing sexual excitement. It was decided that if he was castrated he was the type of dog who would put on an enormous amount of weight. A course of Megestrol Acetate removed the problem. At four years old he is a slim and fit dog, but periodically the bad behaviour returns and it is necessary to treat him. Now, when he starts making amorous advances to the cat, his owner knows it is time to give him a single tablet that cures the problem! How much better for him to have an occasional tablet than to be going around like an obese seal as a result of being castrated.

THE FEMALE DOG—YOUR DOG ON THE "PILL"

Problems arising from the sexuality of your bitch are associated with the different stages of the breeding cycle. Most bitches may come into season, which is the time when they are fertile and mating can take place, when they are six months old. However, there is a great deal of variation from breed to breed, and even within one breed. It is normal that some bitches can come into season as young as four months or as old as two years! Bitches usually come into season twice a year although sometimes small breeds have more frequent seasons. Large breeds may have intervals of a year or more between seasons.

The long interval between seasons means that there is a long period in which there is no activity of the ovaries of the bitch. Some ten days or more before your bitch comes into season the ovaries become active and the vulva starts to become enlarged. During the season there is blood or blood-stained discharge from the vulva. During this time, which normally lasts up to three weeks, your bitch is fertile and you should take strict precautions to prevent any unplanned mating. When the season ends the discharge will stop and your bitch's vulva will return to its normal size. During the ten to 12 weeks after your bitch has been in season she will undergo all the hormone changes that would occur in pregnancy, even if she is not pregnant. Consequently she may show all the physical or mental signs of pregnancy. After this period she will return to the resting stage and the ovaries remain inactive until just before the next season.

During the inactive period of your bitch's breeding cycle, when there is little female hormone activity, there are no related problems with looking after her.

During the time leading up to her season, when changes within the ovaries lead to a change in the level of hormones, your bitch may become aggressive. Sometimes the aggression may only start when the bitch is actually in season, however it is only a few bitches who do become aggressive with the commencement of a season.

Sometimes the aggressive behaviour will disappear when the season has finished. Frequently the aggression will continue after the season is over. If the aggression shown by your bitch is directly associated with the hormone changes, spaying is the obvious cure. In milder cases you may decide to try to treat the aggression medically, although it seems to be less certain than in a male dog that Megestrol Acetate will control hormone-related aggression in the bitch.

Preventing your bitch from coming into season, for example by using Proligestone injections, may be another way to correct the problem. If the bitch has this kind of aggression problem your veterinarian and trainer/behaviourist will be glad to discuss it and offer the best treatment for the particular circumstances.

When your bitch is in season you must have the proper physical control of her to prevent unwanted breeding.

Please remember that when in season a bitch, who is normally content to remain in her own garden, will often go to extreme lengths to escape and seek a male dog. Do make sure that your garden and other areas where your bitch is kept are entirely secure.

It is also very important to ensure that dogs can not get in reach of her. Her scent can be carried through the air, encouraging dogs to visit, so you

A RIPE OLD AGE. Dogs that are neutered usually live longer because the risk of cancer of the reproductive organs is eliminated. Photo by K. Taylor.

may decide to apply a little lotion with a strong smell, such as oil of citronella, to disguise this. Strong disinfectant, put around gates and paths, may also discourage visiting males. If a dog does get to your bitch, none of these measures will prevent mating, so if you take her out when she is in season avoid areas that are frequented by other dogs and keep her on a lead *all the time*.

If your dog is accidentally mated it is well worth consulting your veterinarian immediately. There are injections that can prevent her from conceiving if given soon after mating. However, do not rely on this as a means of birth control. The injections can have undesirable side effects and should not be given repeatedly.

Again Proligestone can be used to prevent her from coming into season. An ongoing programme of injections can be used to prevent breeding throughout her life. One advantage to this is that your bitch does not put on excessive weight and will not suffer from hormone-related urinary incontinence, which can occur with spaying. However, although the risk may be reduced, your bitch can still suffer from diseases of the womb as she grows older.

Remember that there are far more unwanted puppies in this world than there are homes and it is irresponsible to let your bitch breed without proper planning.

I HAVE MY EYE ON YOU. In order to prevent unwanted breeding, your dog should always be supervised when outdoors, and your yard should be secure from wandering members of the opposite sex. Photo by R. Smith.

SAVE A LIFE. Before breeding your dog, consider the welfare of the puppies—will they all have loving homes? Photo by I. Francais.

The normal length of pregnancy is nine weeks. Even if your dog is not pregnant, she may show all the signs of being so: she may put on weight, her milk glands may develop and become full of milk and she may become possessive about toys and other objects. Towards the end of the nine weeks she may seek to make a nest either in her own bed or elsewhere. These symptoms of false pregnancy can be distressing for both you and your bitch.

However, both physical and psychological symptoms of false pregnancy are usually treated easily using hormone therapies or homoeopathy. Frequently, preventing your bitch from coming into season by using Proligestone will prevent a false pregnancy. It is rarely necessary to take the drastic action of spaying your bitch.

The list of possible complications of the breeding cycle makes alarming reading. It is very unlikely that your bitch will suffer from any of them and even more unlikely that they will be severe. It is a good idea to let your bitch have her first season normally and see whether she has any problems. This will allow her to reach her physical, psychological and physiological maturity. If there is a problem arising from her first or from a later season, do seek appropriate professional advice.

WHATEVER YOUR VIEWS ON NEUTERING, PLEASE ONLY ALLOW YOUR DOG TO BREED WITH PROPER PLANNING.

Health Insurance

HEDGING YOUR BETS!

It is very easy to take the continued good health of your puppy for granted. The vast majority of puppies will grow up to be healthy young dogs without any need for professional veterinary treatment for illness or injury. However, illness or an accident can happen without warning and good treatment can be very expensive. Insurance to pay veterinary fees is available at a reasonable cost and is surely a small price to pay for peace of mind. Most insurance policies will also cover you for other problems, as well as veterinary fees. For example they may pay for accidental damage caused by your pet (third-party liability) or boarding charges for your dog if you have to go to hospital yourself. Many people, not having made an insurance claim, will stop their dog's insurance after a few years. Later they are likely to regret this as the older or geriatric dog is far more likely to need veterinary attention.

BEWARE

Many insurance companies exclude certain so-called "dangerous" breeds from their third-party liability cover. Insurance companies may consider Rottweilers, German Shepherd Dogs and especially Pit Bull Terriers in this category.

I'M COVERED. Health insurance for your dog is a good idea, especially during the later years when dogs tend to need more veterinary attention. Photo by J. Waite.

Rabies

Historically the most serious danger from dog bites has been rabies transmitted by the bite of an infected animal. The World Health Organisation estimates that over 15,000 people world-wide die from rabies each year.

It is endemic in Europe and the Americas, where 175,000 people are treated annually after possible exposure.

The last case in England was in 1902, thanks to rigid controls on the entry of animals and their confinement in quarantine for six months. Similar restrictions have excluded rabies from Australia, New Zealand, Iceland and Japan. However, it must be borne in mind that these are islands with a single legislative authority, making control much easier, as has been seen in Hawaii where a 120-day quarantine period is in force. Only some of those attacked by a rabid dog or wild animal go on to develop the disease and this can usually be prevented by effective treatment within one or two days of being bitten. The wound must be cleansed with disinfectant and the dead tissue excised, followed by a course of protective vaccine.

Once established, rabies is one of the most horrific of all diseases and almost invariably fatal.

The virus attacks the central nervous system of the victim to produce a classical, clinical picture, where days of behaviour like a wild animal can alternate with days of clarity and terror. One of the most distressing features is an intense sense of thirst, even sight or sound of water can induce a violent spasm of the respiratory muscles with an intense feeling of panic. No one who has experience of such suffering would contemplate any relaxation of the present quarantine laws in non-endemic areas until infection has been stamped out elsewhere. Travellers to an endemic area and workers exposed to risk can be vaccinated beforehand, whilst vaccination of pet dogs offers limited protection. It must be emphasised, however, that dogs are not the only carriers as rabies can be spread by many wild animals, especially foxes, and once introduced to an urban population rabies can spread rapidly. The French are taking the lead in reducing the risk of rabies in Europe. They offer financial inducement for the elimination of foxes and they are also introducing food baited with the vaccine. Such is the controversy and legislative jungle world-wide that owners concerned with travelling between countries or states with their dogs should consult their veterinarian or health department.

Your Worries about Hip Dysplasia

Unfortunately many of our dogs suffer from diseases that are inherited. Hip dysplasia is probably the best known of these diseases. It occurs in a very large number of different breeds.

Hip dysplasia arises from the incorrect development of the hip. The ball and socket do not fit together properly. The development of this sophisticated joint in the puppy is complicated, and it follows that the inheritance of the disease is also complicated.

There are now programmes that have been developed to reduce the incidence and eliminate the problem from most affected breeds. It involves X-raying the hips of dogs and bitches intended for breeding when they are over a year old. These X-rays are examined by a panel of expert veterinary surgeons. With the aid of geneticists, scoring systems have been devised to express the degree of deformity which may be present. By breeding only from dogs with a low score and

BRITISH VETERINARY ASSOCIATION/KENNEL CLUB HIP DYSPLASIA SCHEME. An example of a scoring system for determining the degree of deformity of hip dysplasia.

Film quality: Satisfactory/too thin/too dark/extraneous marks
Position: Satisfactory/titled laterally left/right/femora not sufficiently extended/femora not evenly extended

HIP JOINT	Right	Left
Norberg		
Subluxation		
Cranial acetabular edge		
Dorsal acetabular edge		
Cranial effective acetabular rim		
Acetabular fossa		
Caudal acetabular edge		
Femoral head/neck exostosis		
Femoral head recontouring		
TOTALS (max possible 53 per column)		

Total Score (max possible 106)

I HEREBY CERTIFY that the above-named animal was examined under the rules of the BVA/KC Hip Dysplasia Scheme

on _____ (date)   Signed _____ (Scheme Secretary)

Signed _____ (Scrutineer)

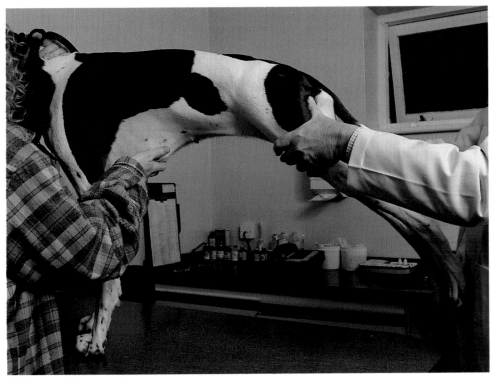

ROUTINE HIP EXAMINATION. Hip dysplasia arises when the surfaces of the dysplastic joint are deformed and do not move over each other correctly. Photo by R. Hutchings.

certainly from dogs with a score below the breed average, the incidence of the disease is reduced.

Symptoms of hip dysplasia are varied. Your dog may become lame in the hind legs or may walk in a peculiar way that is difficult to define. Definitive diagnosis is made by taking X-rays. In very bad cases the X-rays may show obvious disease in the young puppy. In many cases it may only be possible to say whether hip dysplasia is present or not by examining the X-rays taken after your dog is over two years old. By this time the joint has finished developing.

Management and treatment of the disease may vary considerably and must be tailored to suit each individual case. It may be necessary to operate at an early stage to relieve the considerable pain which occurs in bad cases. It may be possible to avoid pain by controlling exercise or it may be necessary to ensure that the dog exercises to prevent the joints from "seizing up".

The surfaces of the dysplastic joint do not move over each other correctly because they are misshapen. As well as causing pain, this causes a considerable amount of arthritis to develop. This can be controlled using anti-inflammatory drugs, which may have to be given continually, and in many cases the symptoms of hip dysplasia respond well to homoeopathy or acupuncture.

Treatment of hip dysplasia is complicated and difficult, each case needing individual attention from your veterinarian.

Caring for the Older Dog

MINIMISING COMMON AILMENTS

Sadly our dogs, like us, grow older and with age various problems can arise. We should be prepared to recognise and adjust to these changes. In reality, they begin to occur somewhere between five and seven years old, depending on the type and breed of dog. Deterioration can occur in any of the body organs or systems. One of the most obvious areas is the mouth; the development of plaque on the teeth can lead to infection and gum disease. Your dog may develop arthritis or diseases of the heart and circulatory system. Tumours and cancer are more common in the older dog.

An increasing number of veterinary practices now operate specific geriatric programmes aimed at helping with the problems of the older dog. Even without one of these programmes, it is a good idea to seek an overall examination of your dog when he has his annual vaccination. At the same time you can discuss with your veterinarian any changes in your dog's behaviour or physical condition. From this examination and discussion he will be able to advise whether your dog should have any further examinations, tests or treatment.

Early recognition and treatment of conditions arising from aging can slow, or even prevent, deterioration in your dog's health. Obviously the better his health, the better is the quality of his life and the greater your enjoyment of his company. However, over a period of time, treatment of the elderly dog can prove to be very costly. Insuring for the cost of veterinary fees when your dog is young and well, and keeping up the insurance policy throughout his life, can remove the burden of paying expensive fees when he is older. The older dog has had time to become a real member of the family. His character has developed, and he has become a treasured part of your life. You both deserve to enjoy each other's company for as long as possible.

TEETH AND GUMS

One of the most common problems with the older dog is deterioration of the teeth and mouth. Plaque can build up on the teeth, penetrate the gums and allow the gums to become infected. This produces a painful inflammation of the gums and if not treated, infection of the roots of the teeth will occur. Frequently, by the time a dog with a tooth problem, is presented to a veterinarian the gums and teeth are so badly infected that it is impossible to save the teeth, and they have to be extracted.

You can do a lot to help preserve your dog's teeth and keep him free of discomfort and pain. We all see our dog's teeth when handling, grooming and playing with him (hopefully in the friendliest possible context!). Look for the telltale signs of brown discoloration of the teeth. This is the plaque beginning to develop. Make a practice of looking at the big teeth at the back of his mouth not just the teeth at the front. The big crushing molar teeth at the back of the mouth and their surrounding gums are often the worst areas for dental disease.

You can help preserve your dog's teeth by ensuring that they are kept clean and that your dog uses them regularly. Most dogs swallow their food with very little chewing, so the teeth are not properly exercised. Providing things to chew can help clean the teeth. Raw beef bones can be provided, but these are messy and some dogs' stomachs cannot tolerate them. A good range of artificial bones and chews which have been designed to be enjoyed by your dog and to clean his teeth are available at your pet shop, the Nylabone® being an excellent example. You can also clean your dog's teeth with a brush and special toothpaste, which is attractive to dogs. These are available from pet shops and veterinarians. It is a good idea to start cleaning your dog's teeth when he is quite young. This will train him to accept the procedure as a normal part of life. Many dogs enjoy having their teeth cleaned. They enjoy the attention and the toothpaste tastes good!

AGING GRACEFULLY. The older dog is subject to many health problems that accompany aging. Regular veterinary visits are imperative at this stage of your dog's life. Photo by R. Hutchings.

YOUNG AT HEART. Heart trouble in the older dog can usually be treated if detected early enough. Photo by R. Hutchings.

HEART AND CIRCULATION

Dogs do not have the same problems with coronary heart disease that plague people. However, their hearts do age. The valves may start leaking, causing a heart murmur or the action of the heart may become irregular.

The arteries, which supply blood to all parts of the body, also deteriorate. They may lose their elasticity and the supply of blood becomes less efficient. This not only puts the heart under greater strain, it means that the various internal body organs cannot perform their functions properly. Often leg muscles are affected and the legs, particularly the hind legs, become weak.

All these problems can be largely overcome if detected early. There are very good treatments available. They can be given over long periods of time and are in no way detrimental to your dog because of side effects.

KIDNEYS

Kidneys are other organs that frequently deteriorate as your dog grows older. All through life they are subjected to various assaults from infections or from doing their job of ridding the body of harmful substances. Mostly, in the young healthy dog, there is no obvious evidence that kidney tissue has been harmed. However, it is not possible for the body to replace kidney tissue which has been destroyed. There comes a time when there is not enough kidney tissue left to get rid of all the waste products of the body and your dog's body tries to adapt and get rid of accumulating waste products by increasing the volume of urine excreted. More water is needed and your dog begins to drink a lot. Although appetite may be increased, he will start to lose weight.

Treatment consists of dieting your dog so that the minimum of waste products are produced by the body. Medicines that can give the kidneys additional help when necessary may be given. Kidney transplants or ongoing dialysis programmes are not really practical alternatives in veterinary medicine at present. Clearly, early treatment of kidney problems allows a much greater chance of improving and prolonging your dog's life.

DIABETES MELLITUS (SUGAR DIABETES)

Diabetes mellitus is another

condition that may develop in the older dog, producing symptoms of excess thirst, wasting of the body and increased appetite. It is less common than kidney disease. It is most important that the cause of the symptoms is established correctly. It is necessary to consult your veterinarian for diagnosis and treatment. There are also rarer diseases that can cause similar symptoms.

Diabetes mellitus occurs because there is a shortage, or complete absence, of insulin in the body. Insulin is a substance produced by the pancreas that controls the amount of sugar in the blood. Lack of insulin allows the blood sugar to increase and the excess sugar is eliminated by the kidneys. The increased kidney activity increases the loss of water in the urine and drinking increases to compensate. At the same time wasting occurs and appetite increases to compensate for the loss of sugar.

Treatment consists of careful dieting to reduce the excessive loss of sugar through the blood and urine and to give insulin when necessary to control the blood-sugar levels. This can only be done with the proper advice and help from your veterinarian.

LOCOMOTOR SYSTEM

Being able to move around freely is an essential part of your dog's life. As your dog grows older you may find that he becomes reluctant to move. This may be due to pain because of arthritis or it may be because he no longer has the strength in his legs to move about with confidence, when there is weakness with no pain, he may stagger or fall over if he tries to move quickly.

Arthritis is a painful inflammation of the joints. It may affect one or many of the joints in the body. Normal wear and tear over a long period is the principal cause of arthritis in the healthy dog. Injury or congenital deformities, such as hip dysplasia, can produce arthritis in specific joints. As with people, some dogs develop arthritis when they are quite young and it remains a problem throughout their lives.

Conventional treatment consists of giving drugs to relieve the pain and reduce the inflammation. It may be necessary to give these drugs for long periods of time or permanently. Prolonged use of these drugs can have undesirable side effects. Physiotherapy can also be used to help the problem. Arthritic dogs often respond extremely well to homoeopathy or acupuncture and it is worth considering these alternatives so that the prolonged use of anti-arthritic drugs can be avoided.

It is essential to consult your veterinarian to obtain an accurate diagnosis of the extent of your dog's arthritis and to get advice on the best way to manage and treat the condition. For example, you can discuss the amount of exercise your dog should have. As time goes by the extent of the condition may alter and treatment may need to be changed. Arthritis is a treatable condition; it may not be possible to produce a complete cure, but it is possible to help the arthritic dog to have a happy and comfortable life.

Weakness of the legs can have a variety of causes. Generally the hind legs are the worst affected. Although muscles can waste away as part of the normal aging process, very often there is an underlying problem. Poor circulation to the hind legs can cause weakness in the muscles which, because they cannot be used properly, deteriorate rapidly. Some lesions, such as arthritis in the back, or a partially prolapsed disc, can affect the nerve supply to the muscles. Again, because the muscles cannot be used properly, they waste away. There are also inherited problems that can lead to wasting of the legs. Perhaps the most well-known is the German Shepherd Dog syndrome called chronic degenerative radiculomyelopathy (C.D.R.M.).This is a specific disease of German Shepherd Dogs producing progressive incoordination of the hind limbs, loss of feeling in the legs and loss of control of the muscles.

In dealing with leg weakness in the older dog, it is vital that a correct diagnosis is reached. Your veterinarian will recommend suitable treatment. Conventional treatments, homoeopathy and acupuncture all have their place. It is imperative to maintain your dog's mobility for as long as possible in order to preserve the quality of his life.

CANCER

While benign tumours and cancers can occur in young dogs, they are generally much more common in older dogs. We have been very successful in treating older dogs to give them a longer life of high quality. It is in these older dogs that cancer is diagnosed more commonly.

Unfortunately, veterinary medicine has fallen behind human medicine in the treatment of cancer. This is largely due to the very high cost of the specialist equipment and facilities needed for research and treatment. Through combining existing veterinary and medical knowledge it is now becoming possible to use some chemotherapy and radiotherapy in support of the surgical removal of a dog's malignant tumour. Some universities and practices accepting referral cases can provide this service. This kind of treatment can be very costly and insurance to cover the cost of veterinary fees is a real benefit in these cases.

THREE LEGS—NO PROBLEM! Dr. Carruthers and German Shepherd Dog, Rufus, a year and a half after amputation for tumor. Photo by M.J. Connolly.

PLAYTIME. Rufus playing with his Nylabone® Frisbee®. Photo by R. Hutchings.

CAUGHT IT! Photo by R. Hutchings.

Zoonoses

Zoonoses are diseases communicable from animals to humans. All pets and their owners can host countless germs, worms and other pests that infest them and then are passed from one another.

The largest of all the medical textbooks are those on human infectious diseases, which spread through kissing, coughing, handling one another's food, bad sanitation and sex. We can infect other animals in contact just as they can pass their own parasites to us. The closer the intimacy the greater the risk and this danger can only be reduced by proper hygiene.

PEOPLE AND FLEAS—AN ITCHY SUBJECT

The hair and hide of a dog, as with its owner's, can be a source of trouble. They can attract unwelcome visitors who would like to stay as permanent lodgers if not firmly removed, in this case by your veterinarian or chemist. One such visitor is the flea.

They tend to rest quietly in the carpets and chairs during the day, but wake up for a nibble at night. They may have a favourite pet but are not choosy and, if this is not around, will settle for one of the family who will present themselves at the doctor's office with itchy spots! Cat and dog owners react emotionally to the suggestion that their pet could be infected as mothers react to the diagnoses of head lice in their children, but it is quite common and only important if the bites become infected. Treatment is of the pet.

YOUR RESPONSIBILITY TO PUBLIC HEALTH

The tail end of the dog demands as much discipline and training by the owner as the dog itself as it has to carry out natural functions. It has been estimated that the canine population in the U.K. passes a thousand tonnes of faeces and nearly five million litres of urine every day and much of this will be in the streets, parks and playing fields where the public walk. Apart from any health hazards this is a great inconvenience, to put it mildly. Their urine being a problem only to the power companies as lamp posts are eroded by the chemical contents!

Fouling of pavements and playgrounds presents a major social problem to the public where there are limited green areas where dogs can be exercised and toiletted safely. The result is often the creation of a vocal anti-dog lobby, which demands that they should be banned altogether from public areas. This is a universal problem and some cities have even tried to set up specific toilet areas, but without any great success. In the U.S.A., U.K. and Australia authorities now have statutory responsibility to keep their area free from dog fouling as well as litter and have responded in different ways. Some have banned dogs altogether from parks and beaches or insisted that they are kept on a leash. Common areas where dogs are exercised and children play do present the risk of an unhealthy level of soil contamination with viable eggs. In contrast, in fenced-off areas where dogs have restricted access this level is greatly reduced although it remains high in the unfenced zones. However, beaches are quite safe as the eggs are rapidly killed off by the sea and the sun. In Australia beaches were found to be clear from infection and even in the U.K., where the sun is a rarer but welcome visitor, sand samples were invariably negative. It seems the poor dog is more likely to pick up food poisoning and eye infections, or even swallow a condom from human sewage contamination of the sea than cause any dangers itself. Such restrictions, however, can make life difficult for the owner, especially the elderly and those

BEACH BUOY. Although some laws do not allow dogs on public beaches for fear of *Toxocara* infection, the combination of sun and sea will eradicate any risk. Photo by P. Aze.

whose pet needs a lot of exercise. Even Royal Commissions have been set up to try and resolve the problem and usually it has been possible to work out a reasonable compromise. It is the responsibility of the owner to ensure that their pet does not foul places to the annoyance of others; indoors their puppy is not allowed to mess all over the place, but is trained to relieve itself on newspaper placed on a floor that can be easily cleaned. The same discipline has to be taught out of doors. The local playground or sports field is not the place for their "loo". Owners should not be surprised that people complain when they find their shoes walking dog mess all over their new carpet after a stroll in the park or the local baseball or cricket team has to spend an hour cleaning up the pitch before they can play.

Many local authorities world-wide have appointed dog wardens with the power to report and/or fine on the spot anti-social behaviour by dogs. You could equally well find a ticket pinned to your dog as well as a parking ticket on your car! Dogs tend to develop regular bowel habits, which can be allowed for when planning their walks. Your own garden or unused rough ground is ideal, but not handy for apartment dwellers in city centres where their dogs have to be trained to use a gutter— preferably not near a pedestrian crossing. When horses were used as transport, small boys would trail behind with a bucket and spade to collect the droppings. The responsible dog owner has to follow suit and clean up after his pet.

The latest scientific evidence shows the following facts, which should allay any fears induced by the anti-dog brigade over the risk of *Toxocara canis*:

1) Dogs over the age of six months are largely immune to toxocara; only 5–10% of dogs in the U.K. over this age have been shown to pass eggs in their faeces.

2) Since eggs passed out in the faeces of infected dogs take a minimum of 14 days to become infective, freshly passed faeces is not a risk if promptly cleared away.

WHAT CAN I DO TO ENSURE MY CHILDREN DON'T GET THESE DISEASES?

The answer is "Plenty".

1) Ensure children always wash their hands before they eat.

2) Discourage them from sucking dirty fingers.

3) Don't allow children to play on the ground and eat using their fingers at the same time.

4) Be sure floors where children play are clean.

5) Don't put small children on the entrance floors of public buildings.

6) Always clear up immediately after pets foul the floor/ground.

All this sounds great but does not dispose of the ultimate problem of what to do with the offering once it has been picked up! The average dog owner will either put it, wrapped up, in a

I'M CLEAN. Humans can pass germs to animals just as animals can pass their parasites to us; this risk can be greatly reduced by proper hygiene. Photo by R. Pearcy.

waste bin or take it home to flush down the toilet. Both have their problems.

Most refuse ends up at tips where birds and stray animals feed and could easily pick up infection. The only safe end point is incineration and some local authorities have organised collection points from which pet faeces is taken away for burning.

As might have been expected from French sophistication, they have developed "pooper-scooters", which go around picking up used "pooper-scoops".

The "loo" is not a popular disposal site with the sewage authorities and kennels are prohibited from using this. They have to incinerate the excrement themselves or make special arrangements for its collection. The problem is that toxocara eggs could be picked up by rats in the drainage system or survive on the filter beds and be spread by birds that feed on these or in the slurry that is spread on the farmland.

YOU, YOUR FAMILY AND WORMS— IS THERE A RISK?

Worms are one of the parasites by which all animals—fish, flesh and fowl—can be infested and man is as vulnerable as any. None are friendly and all cause trouble for their host one way or another. Every animal has its own personal worms, but often these worms have developed a complex life cycle during which

NO DOGS ALLOWED? In order to lift the bans restricting dogs in parks and other public places, owners must become more responsible and consistently clean up after their dogs so that children and their dogs can share the same play areas. Photo by I. Francais.

they cross from one species of animal to another. The adult worm inhabits the intestine of one animal where it feeds and lays its eggs, which pass out in the faeces to become tiny embryos that invade the body of a second. There it undergoes a series of stages of development and finally swaps back to the original host species to grow into an adult worm again.

We have the doubtful privilege of having our own personal worms and sharing many with our animals! The threadworm is a common infestation of children and it lives in the large intestine. The gravid female emerges to lay her eggs around the anus. The egg laying activity of the female is irritant and causes the child to scratch itself, lodging the eggs on the fingers and nails where they are transferred to the mouth to infest others and re-infest themselves. Often a whole family becomes involved. In hot climates with poor sanitation there are many more types of worm that a high proportion of the population carries and passes around.

Bilharzia and hookworms, amongst others, pass their eggs in the stools into the soil or water where people bathe. There they hatch into tiny embryos which can wriggle their way into the skin of the next victim as people walk on contaminated soil and bathe in water.

Tapeworms in particular have built up a chain between man and the animals with whom he works or husbands for food, particularly cattle and pigs, but even fish, goats and camels can be involved in some parts of the world. The adult tapeworm can range in length from being quite tiny to being several metres long as in the case of infected cattle. Their body structure is in segments, the topmost sections attaches the worm to the wall of the gut by suckers or hooks and nutrition is sucked through the surface of the lower segments. The end piece is full of eggs and drops out regularly in the faeces to contaminate soil or water where the eggs can survive a long time due to their protective coat. When swallowed by the next animal in the chain, this piece is digested and the tiny embryo within bores through the gut wall into the bloodstream where it spreads around the body via the liver to the lungs and other tissues, especially muscle. Two bigger adult tapes that concern man are shared with cattle and pigs and infestation is common around the world in farming communities. There is one that man shares with cats and dogs through their fleas, but this is unusual. The adult tape occupation is not usually a danger to health. It can, if large, cause some digestive upset and malnutrition, but it is more of an embarrassment when segments appear outside than anything else.

Perpetuation of the chain depends upon two factors, both of which can be eliminated. The farm animal must eat food or graze on land contaminated with human faeces and, in turn, he must eat their uncooked meat infested with the larvae. Tapeworms are a problem for meat eaters but vegetarians have no such problems, though they can pick up other infections from animals.

The dog is often far too easily blamed for worm-related diseases, for, although not in their natural chain, man can act as piggy-in-the-middle by unwittingly picking up the embryo stages. This is a dead end as far as the worm is concerned, but it can cause more trouble than the worm itself when it lodges in the tissues and vital organs. The pig tapeworm larva can do this because their eggs can be regurgitated into the stomach from the person's own adult worm, where they embed under the skin or, more dangerously, in the nervous system. This can lead to epilepsy and brain damage years later, a condition known as trichinosis— now fortunately rare.

Because of close contact with dogs, both as pets and working animals, humans are liable to be caught up with their worm infestations and there are two in particular that are of special importance—a tapeworm echinococcus whose larvae can lead to hydatid disease in farmers, and a roundworm toxocara that pet dogs and cats can spread. The tapeworm is small, but the animal can house hundreds, each shedding a section containing hundreds of eggs every week or two causing massive contamination of the soil which is spread all around by birds, flies and even beetles and ants. The eggs are picked up as the farm animals graze. Cattle seem to have a natural resistance to infection and horses may not be infective to humans. Sheep seem a peculiar carrier. The big danger lies in the embryo stage; when this develops in the intermediate host it does so slowly to form cysts in the liver, lungs and other tissues, which can become very large. Dogs are reinfected by eating raw meat and offal and it has been found that up to a quarter of all farm dogs in some areas of Wales have tapeworm as well as foxhound packs who are fed on raw sheep carcasses. The human infection by the eggs and larvae can be picked up by close contact with their dogs, infected water, uncooked meat and possibly from food contaminated by flies. The danger rests with the embryos and the large cysts that can develop over the years in the liver, lungs and brain, which damage the organ involved and press on vital structures around. This so-called hydatid disease is common in many farming areas around the world, such as the Middle East, South America and Australasia, but is also in certain parts of the United Kingdom, especially South Wales and Scotland where one in ten people have a positive reaction on routine screening of their blood to determine past exposure to infection. Fortunately few go on to develop any clinical signs, but more than 20 new cases in the

MUDBATH. Dogs can easily pick up tapeworm from contaminated soil. Regular worming of your dog along with proper hygiene can help alleviate this problem. Photo by T.B. Chadwick.

U.K. are admitted to the hospital every year, sometimes with fatal outcome. Medical treatment is of limited value and the cysts have to be removed by surgery.

Hydatid disease should be preventable, as its trail is so established by the education and teamwork of all concerned to break the chain. Some ten percent of all sheep for slaughter may show clear evidence of cystic disease on inspection, although usually they are killed as "fat lambs" before this is evident. Ultimate protection involves regular mass worming of all dogs, checking their access to animal carcasses on the farm, monitoring raw meat and offal at the abattoirs and knackers yards, combined with personal hygiene and proper cooking.

The worm infection that has aroused most public concern is toxocara. The adult worm is mainly carried by dogs *(Toxocara canis)*, cats *(Toxocara cati)* and by wild animals, especially the fox. The larvae can cause illness in humans, especially children, who have ingested the infective eggs from soil contaminated by these animals, of whom the pet dog has been held mostly to blame, although determining cause to the fox or dog is impossible. Toxocara was only first linked with human illness in the early 1950s, since then a great deal more information has been built. It is now clear that many of us have picked up infection in our early years, as with tuberculosis, but never suffered in any way and merely built up defences. In Western Europe and the U.K. routine screening tests on adults show positive antibodies in about two percent of the population, over a million overall, but inquiry and follow-up show they did not suffer ill effects at the time of infection nor are likely to do so in the future. Regrettably the anti-dog lobby uses these figures to suggest that this number of people had or will go on to develop illness. This is simply untrue—they merely carry the anti-bodies as is normal with countless diseases. In spite of this level of exposure, toxocariasis is a rare disease and about 110-120 new cases of ocular toxocariasis are identified each year in the whole of the U.K.

Seropositivity

Less than five percent of healthy adults in the U.K. are seropositive or have antibodies to toxocara present in their blood. In the U.S.A. this figure is seven percent and in Eastern Europe it is even higher—greater than ten percent. Australian figures show a wide range, two to eight percent.

Seropositivity means that the affected person has been exposed to toxocara antigens and does not necessarily mean that the person is infected or diseased. There are two stages at which infection may be identified. The first occurs during the initial invasion when an acute allergic reaction may occur in response as the embryonic larvae migrate through the body. This usually involves young children who may run a temperature, with a chesty cough and wheezing, tummy upset with tenderness of the liver— all the sites where the parasite tends to lodge. The symptoms are mild and likely to be labelled a virus infection or food poisoning and the true diagnosis is usually missed. Only rarely is it more serious causing meningitis, convulsions or even heart failure. The natural course is a spontaneous cure, although this can take a year or two. Recovery can be speeded up by appropriate drugs to kill the parasite, but their sudden death can exacerbate the allergic response and this has to be done slowly under steroid cover to reduce the risk.

I CANNOT SEE A PROBLEM.

The most threatening complication of infection results from the predilection of the larvae to settle in and around the eye (ocular toxocariasis) and it is often complaints about some loss of vision, squinting or "seeing light" that first draw attention to infestation. Any part of the eye may house the larvae causing local damage, but it is only in a minority of cases when this is located near the optic nerve disc or the retina becomes severely inflamed that serious damage to sight in the affected eye occurs. One serious consequence of local reaction can be the development of swelling that resembles a malignant tumour and the eyes were removed in error before doctors learned that toxocara could cause a similar picture.

When the problem of eye trouble from toxocariasis is raised, it is often implied that a likely consequence is blindness; this is inaccurate. Many cases will clear up altogether and only a small proportion suffer some permanent loss of vision in a single eye. Medical awareness of the condition and wonder treatment with steroids and laser coagulation surgery has greatly improved the outcome. We are faced with approximately 110-120 new cases of related eye trouble a year in the U.K., far fewer than occur in a single evening from fireworks on Guy Fawkes Night. Both are equally tragic, but to a great extent preventable.

WILL I CATCH A STOMACH BUG FROM MY DOG?

The animal intestine is a favourite site for a great many other forms of life to inhabit. Some make it their home and settle down happily, having worked out a relationship that is mutually beneficial. Like any other good lodger, they pay rent for their stay by helping in food digestion or keeping harmful germs at bay. But many are parasites that feed off their hosts and cause trouble in some form of illness or ill health. They depend for their continual existence on being passed on from one victim to the next and some have developed complex pathways that often involve passage from one species of animal to another. Humans pick up intestinal infections mainly through the food and water they eat and drink, personal contact, poor hygiene and the animals that they farm for food. *Very few are linked with companion animals.* The main exceptions are the roundworm infection that occurs in pet cats and dogs called toxocara and a tapeworm in working farm dogs, which cause hydatid disease. In both cases the human is an unfortunate intermediary and not part of the worm's planned life cycle. Infection from our food remains a problem everywhere and most of us suffer food poisoning from time to time. This is steadily on the increase although it is almost entirely preventable as the causes are well known. Greed, laziness and poor personal hygiene are to blame. Protection lies in our own hands by observing the big "C's"—Care, by those who farm and market our food; Cooking, because all the germs responsible are killed by heat; Cleanliness, by ourselves and those who handle our food.

Food poisoning can be caused by a wide range of germs, of which salmonella and, increasingly, campylobacter are the best known. The source is almost invariably food that is undercooked, reheated or handled by someone who is themselves infected. Apart from turtles and terrapins, which cause salmonella outbreaks through water in their tanks, *pets play little part in the spread of food poisoning.* A few human cases of campylobacter have been traced to infected puppies and kittens, but otherwise pets have a clean sheet. Our dogs can equally suffer from food poisoning, often from being fed left-overs from the fridge that smell too bad to give to the family. Again the most serious germ responsible is salmonella, picked up from eating contaminated food. The reservoirs are poultry and cattle who do not suffer themselves but can pass on their infection in their meat and dairy products, such as eggs and milk. Possibly a third of cattle and poultry is infested mainly through the cheap imported animal foodstuffs they are fed. A great deal of our meat is frozen "fresh". Salmonella can survive happily in the deep freeze and when it is warmed up to a suitable temperature it will start to multiply. Many of the outbreaks are due to meat, especially chicken, that has been fully defrosted and is left uncooked in the middle. Infected raw eggs are also a menace.

So apart from asking "What germs do our dogs give us?", we

ALLERGIC? If someone in your family is sensitive to dog hair, a Poodle may be the dog for you. Unlike most other breeds, they do not shed their coats. Photo by I. Francais.

should also be considering "What germs do we give our dogs through lack of care and poor hygiene?"

ASTHMA AND ALLERGIES

As we have been learning to control many of the infections and other diseases to which humans are prone, another group has been steadily increasing in frequency causing great discomfort and suffering to those concerned. They are the allergy conditions that result from an over-reaction by the body's natural defences.

Partly these are the white cells in the blood and lymphatic system that kill or ward off any live invaders. Other cells spread all around our body and release chemical substances in response to foreign materials. In the average person this response is well controlled, but some people react out of proportion to any real danger. Often this is an inherited tendency and they become hyper-sensitive and over-reactive to substances that would normally be ignored. In extreme cases a wasp sting or a particular food or a drug such as a simple aspirin can precipitate a violent general reaction that can be life threatening. Usually the irritants to which people become over-sensitive are contaminants in the air they breathe. When the lining membranes of the eyes and nose over-react to pollens, they become swollen and congested causing hay fever, whilst in lungs spasms of the swollen respiratory tubes lead to asthma. Hay fever tends to be seasonal, related to pollens and grasses in the spring or summer and mildews in the autumn. Asthma is less so as this is often in response to the mites that are found in house dust and bedding. These allergic states have increased manifold over recent years, especially in towns, and more than two million people in the U.K. are asthmatics. The underlining reasons for this are not certain, but they are seldom only vulnerable to a simple factor and much of the blame has to be attributed to the increased pollution of our streets, places of work and especially homes to which many of the irritants have been introduced. The doctor called to an asthmatic at home will often find the patient with an inhalant in one hand and a cigarette in the other and the house reeking of hair spray and deodorants to which he may be equally sensitive.

One of the initiators that can bring on an asthma attack in a sufferer is animal dander, especially cats, but the hair and hide of the hound or any other animal can be responsible.

In general there is not a great deal that can be done about this and if the whole family shares this allergy, it may have to keep a goldfish as its pet. When susceptible friends come to dinner, it is safer to separate your dog or cat from the visitors for the evening than to risk precipitating an acute asthma attack.

This may seem rather depressing for any prospective dog owner, but he or she should keep a sense of

HERE A HAIR, THERE A HAIR. The Shetland Sheepdog is one breed that sheds a great deal; asthma sufferers and people who are allergic to dog hair should be careful before choosing this dog as a pet. Photo by R. King.

proportion. Dogs are probably the safest as well as the most companionable pets.

THE MINIMAL RISK OF OTHER COMMUNICABLE DISEASES FROM OUR DOGS

One of the parasites that enjoys preying on animals is the fungus, man having the privilege of being one of its favourite hosts. Some select hairy and sweaty parts, such as the scalp; the feet, causing "athletes foot"; the private parts, where ringworm is one of the five infections that compose the seaman's original "full house"— crotch rot, crabs, scabies, gonorrhoea and syphilis.

Ringworm likes a surface of non-hairy areas, feeding on the dead layers of skin. The actual advance is a slow-creeping, scaly, red, irregular border, whilst the centre heals up. It is a classical picture that is easily cleared up when diagnosed but doctors will look for the origin of infection, which can be a wide range of sources, animal or vegetable. Sometimes this could be a pet cat or dog and they have to be checked.

Another common world-wide disease that can infect most animals, including dogs and man, is leptospirosis and it is caused by a wriggly germ that is spread from host to host, mainly through water contaminated by infected urine. The main source is rats. Leptospirosis was mainly an occupational hazard for coal miners, workers in the sewage and water industries and soldiers in the army. Now the pattern has changed and both dairy and fish farmers are equally at risk. Many cases occur through fresh water swimming pools and water sports. Although the main source of contamination is rats, cattle are now a common source and contamination can cause abortions in cows with infected end products, a danger for veterinarians and meat inspectors. The infection in man is called Weil's disease and the strain of germs carried by rats is a dangerous one causing jaundice, bleeding and kidney damage, which can prove fatal. Dogs are a relatively minor source of infection and the particular strain they can pass on causes a much more benign condition usually limited to a feverish illness of which the one real complication is a mild form of meningitis with complete recovery.

There are two infections, in hot dry climates and when bitten by insects, that can travel between man and dogs or rodents. The first of these is leishmaniasis, endemic in many areas including the Mediterranean, Middle East and Southern Russia, where over one million cases occur every year. Dogs are the main reservoir and the sand fly is the transmitter.

Another infection in the Mediterranean area is tick typhus, domestic pets again acting as a reservoir from which the germ is passed to humans by ticks. A few infected animals have been picked amongst the 400 or so that pass through quarantine here each year, but there is no risk held in the absence of the necessary vector insects.

First Aid for Dogs

The principal aims of first aid are:

1) Preserve life

2) Reduce pain and discomfort and prevent further damage where possible.

In a real emergency always telephone for veterinary assistance.

APPROACHING THE ANIMAL

The correct method of approaching and restraining the animal is vital to prevent it from inflicting further damage on itself and injury to the first-aider. WARNING: Injured dogs can be dangerous—approach with caution. The approach must always be made slowly, calmly, confidently, quietly and sympathetically. If it is not your own dog and looks unfriendly, do not proceed. Call for expert advice.

Action

Even if it is possible to approach the animal it will need restraining before attempting first aid. If there is no major injury to the head region this is best done with a tape muzzle. If the animal is conscious and mobile it may be possible to coax it into the back of a car. If the dog cannot move, has collapsed, or is unconscious, it should be placed on a blanket or coat as gently as possible. It is preferable to have two people involved if possible so that the second person can keep the dog under control during the journey.

SERIOUS INJURY

If an animal is seriously injured due to a car accident or fall, it is vital that you arrange immediately for veterinary attention. However, it is important to be able to assess the animal's condition in order to give an accurate report.

1) Is the dog breathing? Is there any movement in the chest and abdomen?

2) Has it a heartbeat? Feel by putting hand or fingertips on the chest behind the elbow joint.

3) Is it conscious, does it respond to call? Can it see?

4) Having established that the dog is alive, give it a quick external examination. Is the dog sustaining severe blood loss from any wound?

5) Is the dog in shock? This can be life threatening.

Signs: weakness, rapid shallow breathing, cold and clammy gums, lips and tongue, cold paws, rapid heartbeat, glazed eyes, dilated pupils, vomiting. All or some of these signs may be present.

Action

a) Get veterinary help as soon as possible.

b) Artificial respiration is vital; if the animal is not breathing, it will die! Provided that the heart does not stop, artificial respiration can keep an animal

SHOCKED. Rapid heartbeat is one sign that your dog could be in shock. Seek veterinary help immediately. Photo by K. Taylor.

alive for a couple of hours—certainly until you can get professional help. There are three methods:

(i)"Kiss of Life"—Have the head and neck straight forward, (extended—not bunched up). Close animal's mouth and blow regularly into the nose with lips close to the nostrils. This is a suitable method in situations where there is a penetrating wound to the chest, etc. Blow in for three seconds and then pause for two seconds. Repeat continuously.

(ii) Chest Compressions—If possible, lay dog flat on its right side. Have the head and neck straight forward (extended—not bunched up) with the tongue well forward out of the mouth to clear the airway. Place two hands on the chest wall over the ribs and push down firmly to expel the air from the lungs. Immediately release the pressure, allowing the lungs to fill with air. Repeat at five second intervals. Be firm but *not* forceful—do not crush the animal's chest!

(iii) Cardiac Massage—If no heartbeat can be felt (by placing fingers on lower part of chest wall on the left side just behind the front leg), then start rhythmical compressions at half-second intervals simultaneously applied on either side of the rib cage over the area of the heart, along with giving artificial respiration. Continue until the heart beats

THE HEART OF THE MATTER. Dog having an E.C.G. (electrocardiogram) taken. This device detects heart activity. Photo by K. Taylor.

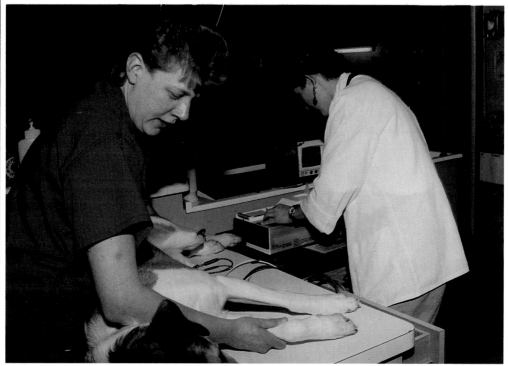

again—if you have no success and no response from the dog, then unfortunately it is probably too late.

c) Keep the animal warm with blanket, coat, newspaper, etc. However, *do not* raise the temperature of the animal much higher than its surroundings, do not place the dog in front of a fire or in electric blankets as this can cause more damage.

d) Keep the animal quiet.

e) Do not give the animal alcohol.

f) Avoid moving the animal when possible and keep shifts and jolts while being carried to a minimum.

CUTS

There are three types you may encounter:

1) Incised—Usually a clean cut from a sharp object (glass, metal, etc), can bleed profusely.

2) Lacerated—A torn irregular wound from barbed wire, road accidents, etc. This will probably bleed slightly less, but is much more likely to get dirty.

3) Puncture—Caused by sharp point from an animal bite, thorn, fish hook etc. These can be nasty; being deep they may heal on the surface but not underneath.

Action

Once again quickly assess the wound, its size and depth. If slight, gently clean in tepid water. Keep an eye on it and seek veterinary advice if you are at all unsure.

Suspected injuries to nerves and tendons are very serious and a vet should be summoned as soon as possible. *Severe bleeding can lead to shock.* It is usually important to stem blood flow, by applying pressure from hand or bandage, until veterinary help can be obtained. In all cases seek veterinary help as soon as possible.

a) Serious cuts in the abdominal area—Do not give anything to eat or drink; and do not wash, as fluid may enter abdominal cavity.

If abdominal organs have protruded on *no* account try to replace them. Try to restrain the dog on its back or firmly keep it on its side. Cover the protruding organs with a large piece of clean gauze or other clean material and bandage in place using a crepe bandage, scarf or similar by passing around the abdomen if possible.

b) Chest wounds from stabbing, impaling, gunshot, etc. If there is a severe wound in the chest region and blood is frothing and/or a sucking sound can be heard, *seal it.* The dog will have difficulty breathing as air may be being sucked in and out of the wound. It should be sealed preferably with sterile lint or gauze, but in an emergency a clean hanky or towel.

Do not use fibred fabric such as cotton wool. Keep the mouth open and forward and *do not* bathe the wound or give anything by mouth.

Frothing blood from the dog's mouth almost certainly indicates internal bleeding.

c) Foreign bodies in wound—If

minor, and on the surface of paws or skin, remove with tweezers. If you do not succeed do not continue to dig, but see a vet.

If there is a foreign body in a deep cut, *do not* remove it as it may make the bleeding worse.

d) Penetrating foreign body in eye, nose, or ear—Do not remove. Seek veterinary advice.

HEAT STROKE

It is vital to remember that dogs should not be left in hot and/or badly ventilated surroundings, such as cars parked in the sun. This can lead to unconsciousness.

(It is prohibited in some American states to leave your dog unattended in a car.)

Action

a) Remove dog to a shady ventilated area.

b) Immediately lower the dog's body temperature by spraying or sponging with cold water. You should notice a marked improvement in the dog's breathing and awareness.

c) Dry in a cool place, have water on hand for the dog to drink. Monitor the dog carefully and be ready to call vet if needed.

If you have to continue a car journey, make sure that the interior temperature has dropped, windows are open and, if necessary, stop regularly to cool the dog.

BURNS

Burns not only damage the skin, they can lead to shock and later on sepsis.

Action

a) Burns caused by fire, boiling oil, liquids, etc. Smother flames with blanket, coat or rug (*do not* use man-made fibres that may melt and worsen the situation). In all cases apply cold water liberally as soon as possible for at least ten minutes. Do not try to pull any burned material away from skin and do not prick any blisters. Do not apply any lotions, potions or creams. It is always wise to seek veterinary advice.

b) Chemical burns—As above. Do not worry about neutralising the corrosive, just apply water, but ensure that the dog does not lick its coat or drink any of the water that has been used to wash it.

c) Electrical burns—Not common, but they could occur if a puppy, for example, chews through a wire. Switch off the current and/or make sure electrical contact is broken before touching the dog. The main danger of this type of contact is the cessation of breathing and heartbeat from muscular spasm. The actual burns look localised at the point of contact, but are often deep. Occasionally there is also a burn at the exit point of the current. If the dog has stopped breathing apply artificial respiration. Check heartbeat and act accordingly. Keep the dog quiet and calm and seek veterinary attention.

STINGS

Wasp and bee stings are very common particularly in the summer months. Symptoms can range from minor irritation to severe restriction of the trachea.

Action

a) If the sting is external and accessible, try to remove stinger with tweezers.

b) Apply cold compress.

c) Give antihistamine treatment if available.

d) If breathing is restricted, your vet must be contacted immediately for an antihistamine injection.

e) If your vet is likely to take some time attending, advice must be sought from him. A tube may have to be put down the throat to aid breathing or in extreme cases an emergency tracheotomy be given.

CHOKING

It is important to realise that a dog with a bone, stick or needle jammed in his throat will be distressed and will need careful handling. The animal may even collapse due to lack of oxygen.

Action

a) Open dog's mouth and quickly attempt to grasp the foreign body with minimum damage to the mouth. This is obviously easier if you have an assistant. On no account push the object further down the

MADE IN THE SHADE. When on outings with your dog, make sure that there is a shady area for him to retreat to avoid sunstroke or heatstroke. Photo by I. Francais.

throat. This will not relieve the problem, it will make it worse.

b) If the foreign body is jammed in the windpipe, such as a small ball, then the dog can be laid on its side on a firm surface. Apply a sudden sharp downward push on the abdomen just behind the last rib. A helper should open the dog's mouth and attempt to grasp the foreign body as it is forced up.

POISON

This can be through ingestion, inhalation or though direct contact with the skin.

Action

a) Ingestion—Immediately wash away as much poison as possible (taking care of yourself if it is corrosive) with tepid water. Cause the animal to vomit if possible, but *do not* do this if the dog is having convulsions, is in a coma, is unable to swallow or if the substance is corrosive (battery acid, ammonia, creosote, bleach, etc.) or is petroleum based.

Call the vet for advice on what to give the dog internally to neutralise the substance. Intermediate or incorrect use of washing soda, salt or milk can make matters worse.

b) Inhalation—Remove the dog to a source of fresh air and call vet.

c) Contact with skin—Remove as much poison as you can with warm water, paper towels, etc. *Do not* use solvents, such as paint stripper or turpentine, as these can be corrosive.

Contact a veterinarian if you are in any doubt, or if the dog is showing abnormal signs that could indicate poisoning.

Try and prevent the dog from licking its coat.

SNAKE BITES

The main snake bites that are potentially dangerous to dogs are large Rattlesnakes, Coral Snakes, large Cottonmouths and many Asian and African Cobras; in Australia, Brown Snakes (Western Brown or Gwardar and Dugite), Western Tiger Snake or Norne, Mulga, Death Adders, Taipan.

It is essential whenever possible to identify the variety of snake, or at least tell your vet its colour and size, in order that the correct anti-venom be given.

Clinical signs vary: local swelling, weakness, lack of muscular coordination, vomiting, salivation, blood in urine, dilated pupils, breathing difficulty, defecation.

Action

a) Do not try to suck the venom out. (This is likely to poison you.)

b) Do not apply a tourniquet.

c) Keep the dog still; movement will cause faster circulation of the venom.

d) Wash affected area.

e) Contact veterinarian. Time is of the essence.

Authors' note: The above points are emergency procedures and are no substitute for veterinary attention.

KEEP YOUR DOG HEALTHY AND SAFE. There are many dangers that dogs face; dogs are like children and need to be carefully supervised. Photo by Mrs. H.J. Wilkinson.

Alternative Medicine

"With the growing interest in Alternative Medicines for humans it is only natural that people should now start to look at holistic medicines for their pets."
  Hilary Self

ACUPUNCTURE FOR DOGS
by J. Nicol, MRCVS

Acupuncture in animals started about 5000 years ago in China as a branch of Chinese medicine, a large part of which is still based on ancient herbal remedies.

Acupuncture is largely empirical in that it has developed over the centuries from the experience of practitioners. It is based on the theory of Yin and Yang which holds that every object or phenomena in the universe consists of two opposite aspects, which are at once in conflict and in interdependence; further, that this relationship between Yin and Yang is the universal law of the material world, the principle and source of the existence of myriads of things and the root cause for the flourishing and perishing of things. This theory mainly expounds the opposition, interdependence, inter-consuming-supporting and inter-transforming relationship of Yin and Yang. These relationships are extensively used in traditional Chinese medicine to explain the psychology and pathology of the body and serve as a guide to diagnosis and treatment in clinical work. This interdependent relationship means that each of the two aspects is the condition for the other's existence and that neither of them can exist in isolation. For instance, without daytime there would be no night; without excitation there would be no inhibition. Hence, it can be seen that Yin and Yang are at once in opposition and in interdependence. They rely on each other for existence, co-existence in a single entity.

In Chinese medicine it is believed that vital energy or "chi" flows through a series of channels or meridians which have connections from the surface of the skin to internal body organs.

Disease is thought to be an interruption in the flow of energy through these meridians resulting in an imbalance of Yin and Yang. The object of treatment is to select the correct acupuncture points to reverse the imbalance.

There is now much scientific evidence as to the effectiveness of acupuncture and to the psychological basis for this. It is known for instance that if certain points are stimulated, opioid substances known as endorphins are released. Similarly, it has been shown that needling certain points will change beta brain waves to alpha waves, which is the resting state of the brain. There are many other measurable phenomena that occur in the body under the stimulation of acupuncture, which are leading to a greater understanding of the mechanisms of pain control.

Stimulation of acupuncture points can be achieved in a number of ways, the most common of course is by dry needling with stainless steel needles of fine gauge. The first principle in successful needle therapy is to achieve a state of "te chi", which in Chinese means that the needle has contacted the "chi" or vital energy and this must be manipulated if therapy is to be effective. It means that there is a deep feeling of soreness, heaviness, numbing or tingling. In animals "te chi" responses are seen as uneasiness, stamping the ground, swinging the tail and local muscle twitching at or around the insertion site. Cold beam lasers are now quite popular as a means of stimulating points, largely because the procedure is painless and does not take long to perform. However, the laser beam can only penetrate a short distance in the tissue and therefore is of limited value in heavily muscled areas and in the writer's experience is less effective than needling. In chronic conditions such as hip dysplasia, where a favourable result has been obtained by needling, a long-term effect can be achieved by implanting gold or silver beads into the acupuncture points. Many veterinary acupuncturists use injections of small quantities of fluid to stimulate acupuncture points, which of course saves a considerable amount of time since

POINTS OF VIEW. Acupuncture in dogs can be used to treat such conditions as hip dysplasia and heart disease. Photo by M. Fellows.

several points can be injected in a couple of minutes instead of dry needling for approximately 20 minutes. Electrical stimulation of the needles is often used for acute painful conditions and for some stages of paralysis.

The main indications for acupuncture in dogs are for some skin conditions, pain control as in osteo-arthritis or in neurogenic pain, injuries from various causes, cervical, thoracic and lumber disc problems as well as many medical conditions such as chronic diarrhoea, heart disease, liver problems and some forms of epilepsy.

There are very few conditions that will not benefit from acupuncture especially if used early in the treatment programme rather than as a last resort. It is often an alternative to premature euthanasia in dogs.

BACH FLOWER THERAPY

Probably Bach Flower remedies are the most complex form of alternative medicine with which to come to terms. It is difficult to grasp the psychological concepts of the Bach Flower method of treating illness.

In 1930 Dr. Edward Bach, a successful bacteriologist and homoeopathic doctor, gave up his Harley Street practice to look for a simple and natural method of treating illness. He took the view that "there are no diseases, only sick people". He introduced a new form of diagnosis based on negative feelings rather than the symptoms of disease. There is no scientific explanation as to why Bach Flower remedies work.

Bach wrote that the remedies "are able, like beautiful music or any glorious uplifting thing which gives us inspiration, to raise our very natures, and bring us nearer to our souls, and by that very act, bring us peace and relieve our sufferings". He argued that disease arises because one's personality is not in harmony with one's soul, the real self. However, it may be the soul that is in a negative state. For example, greed is the negative soul quality of love.

Bach used negative soul states to make his diagnosis. These states are to be flooded away with "higher, harmonious energy waves". Bach used flowers to produce these effects. By placing the leaves from the plant on his tongue, he was able to detect their effect. It was important that the flowers should be growing in completely natural conditions and not be cultivated. The flowers should be picked when they are fully mature, and should be processed as soon as possible. The remedies are now produced at the Bach Flower Centre in England and distributed throughout the world.

Diagnosis for Bach Flower Therapy is based on the very deep philosophical concepts of psychology, which we have described briefly. It is difficult enough to do this with people— even more difficult with your dog!

Some people are able to reach a diagnosis intuitively. More commonly it is necessary for the therapist to discuss and observe your dog's behaviour with you. He will then recommend one or more remedies to return your dog to proper health.

In veterinary medicine there appears to be a far greater success rate when Bach Flower Therapy is used for behavioural problems rather than in specific diseases. Perhaps this is a reflection of the difficulty in arriving at the correct treatment. Our assessment of behavioural problems may be more accurate than our ability to detect psychological problems in a dog that behaves normally but is ill.

RESCUE REMEDY

Rescue Remedy is probably the most well known of the Bach Flower remedies. It is not a single

BACK TO BARK. The Bach Flower Remedy, which uses all-natural methods, has proven successful in treating behavioural problems in dogs. Photo by T.B. Chadwick.

remedy in itself but a combination of five remedies.

Spectacular effects are achieved after injury. It prevents or removes the symptoms of shock or bruising. In people it will often overcome the effects of mental stress. It can be used whenever your dog is injured by placing a few drops in the mouth and will not interfere with any subsequent treatment that may be necessary.

HERBAL SUPPLEMENTS FOR DOGS
by Hilary Self

Herbs have been used for animals and humans alike for hundreds if not thousands of years. They are a gentle form of treatment that work in the truly holistic way of getting to the cause of the problem rather than just tackling the resulting symptoms as conventional medicine often does. We owe it to our canine friends to do the very best for them—herbs, along with diet, grooming, exercise and training can help to give our dogs a healthy and happy life.

Herbs like all living things contain ingredients that have various actions. These actions can be highly beneficial to dogs, who in the wild would source them through their omnivorous diet. (How often do you see dogs eating various grasses?)

Dogs of all ages can benefit from the feeding of herbal supplements. Unfortunately modern food processing systems often mean that many of our convenience dog foods are lacking in vital minerals, vitamins and trace elements necessary for healthy bodily systems. Herbs have a variety of actions that can improve and support the digestive, nervous, circulatory and lymphatic systems of the body.

Often the first signs of deficiencies will be seen in the condition of the coat and skin. Scurf, eczema and loss of hair are probably the most common complaints faced by today's dog owners. It is obviously vital to maintain top grooming and beauty care. However, the condition of the dog's internal systems are reflected in the quality of its coat and skin, hence the old adage "cold, wet nose— healthy dog". Every dog owner knows the benefits of sulphur for blood cleansing. Marigold flowers are rich in sulphur and, with the addition of other herbs that cleanse the blood, improve digestion and strengthen the coat. The dog is able to support a healthy coat and skin and thereby avoid these conditions.

For the young and fast-growing dog, herbs rich in vitamins and minerals can be given to ensure strong healthy development of the nervous and muscular-skeletal system.

For the dog in middle life and particularly working dogs, herbs that will support the digestive, lymphatic and circulatory systems are needed to ensure that conditions such as arthritis, liver and kidney disorders and rheumatism are not allowed to develop.

Bitches suffering from hormone imbalances that may display signs of aggressiveness or suffer from phantom pregnancies can be helped with hormone balancing herbs that will gently act on the pituitary gland helping it to restore the body's hormone levels to normal.

For the elderly dog who may already have such conditions as kidney and liver disorders or arthritis, herbs such as nettle, clover, comfrey and devil's claw will help to cleanse the blood, support the lymphatic system, reduce inflammation and restore mobility to elderly joints. All this without the risk of side effects and toxic damage that can so often result when strong drugs such as steroids are used.

When training a dog, the job is made so much easier if the animal is healthy, happy and in good condition. Often this ideal situation does not exist; indiscriminate breeding can produce dogs that are nervous and high strung. This makes the job of training that much harder. Herbs that have a calming and soothing effect such as valerian, chamomile and scullcap can often help in these situations by soothing and strengthening the nervous system. The dog learns to relax and enjoy its training. It comes to accept new handlers more readily. These herbs have been found to be particularly useful when dealing with dogs that have been badly treated and have subsequently lost confidence in humans. The new owner is often faced with the difficulty of getting close enough to the dog for a bond of trust and friendship to develop. By using calmative and nervine herbs the dog becomes more accessible and starts to relax, making it easier to handle and less likely to take fright. Herbs used as part of a dog's every day diet can help to alleviate a wide variety of problems.

HOMOEOPATHY
by Richard Croft

Homoeopathy provides a speedy and effective method of helping animals that is absolutely safe and easy to administer without side effects.

Animals, in general, respond well to homoeopathic treatments. Some people have tried to explain the success of homoeopathy by suggesting that its effectiveness depends upon the psychology of the patient, which means that they believe that they will be cured so their minds condition their bodies to respond. This obviously cannot be true of animals. Neither can the animal assist the practitioner by telling him how he feels and the diagnosis must be made on the observations made by both the practitioner and the owner.

One of the reasons that homoeopathic products are so safe is the method used in preparing the substance by progressive dilution. This substance, undiluted, given in large doses would in fact cause the symptoms.

Dilution is usually done in steps of one part of a substance to 100 parts: 30 c as a potency dilution means that 30 dilutions have taken place, in other words the original substance is diluted to such an extent that there is not a single molecule of the original substance left in the remedy.

The homoeopathic system can be useful when dogs are nervous or excitable and with the help of these products and training much can be achieved. Homoeopathy can also help with non-parasitic skin problems, arthritis and hormonal problems such as false pregnancy. Because homoeopathy is so safe, it is particularly useful where prolonged or repeated treatment is necessary; some conventional medicines used long term may produce undesirable side effects.

The homoeopathic practitioner endeavours to build a multi-dimensional picture of his patient and then matches this picture with proven remedies. Infinitesimal doses of a remedy help the patient's body to heal itself.

USING SPIRITUAL HEALING IN THE TREATMENT OF ANIMALS
by David Sampson

By attuning himself to the animal and to the divine creative force, a healer can channel through to a sick or injured pet or animal a life-giving energy that can sometimes produce quite remarkable help. There is a life-force that motivates all life, but with illness or age, or perhaps misuse, an animal's vitality is lowered and the immune system less able, or even unable, to cope. Also when medication is administered and little response is forthcoming, then it is probable that the energy is too "low" to stir

into action. This is when spiritual healing may help. In a busy healing centre, there is quite often a pet waiting for treatment and this forms a special part of our work. Here are three short cases of healing at work.

Jenny is a large cross-bred, aged 12 years, blind and had not been in good health for quite some time. She lives in Oxford, England, and was brought to see me about a year ago because she was so weak that the end of her life seemed close. She was carried in and set down just inside the waiting room door, so I administered healing to her there. After the laying-on of hands for a few minutes, I felt "something stir" inside her and I thought she may have died. I carried her out to the car and did not think she would survive the night, but the next day the owner was on my doorstep to say that Jenny had slept deeply through the night, had demanded a good breakfast and was now taking quite a long walk. She has come to see me about four times for healing since we first met and remains very well, active and obviously enjoying life—and so are her owners!

Kirsty is a beautiful horse, bred as a "jumper". She became very ill with an infected leg which did not respond to any treatment and the vet decided that he must end her life since she was in great pain. I was asked to see her and at once she seemed to feel the effect of healing. When the veterinarian next called, intending to end Kirsty's life, he was pleased at the substantial improvement in her

AT PEACE WITH THE WORLD. Spiritual healing can offer a lifegiving energy to a sick dog, and provide him the necessary boost to recover. Photo by A. Chen.

condition and was glad for me to continue treatment. I gave her healing about ten times, with good progress each time, until I felt I could help no more. That was eight years ago and Kirsty has since produced three foals and is in fine condition, although her leg is misshapen.

A most beautiful rabbit arrived in a box, looking nearly dead. He was quite famous locally as a desired mate for any doe but for several weeks he would not stir, even for the loveliest of females! The vet could find no illness or injury, and yet he was clearly in a bad way. He would hardly eat anything or move much. As I laid hands on him I was aware that he had an appalling headache and it seemed to move away as I held him. I have not seen him again, but he was completely O.K. by the next morning and has been breeding well since! I imagined him saying "Not tonight, Josephine, I've got a headache!"

In all these cases, was it just that the animals needed life-giving energy and, having received it, their own bodies used it to aid recovery?

Choosing a "User-Friendly" Vet

HAS YOUR VET GOT A GOOD "PETSIDE" MANNER?

How many of us leave our vets' surgery, head spinning, not understanding a single word that has been said? Mind you, vets are not the only people to blame. Try walking into a computer shop, asking a question and seeing if the reply resembles anything of the English language. Or how about the garage mechanic who goes into lengthy details about excessive ohm resistance in your car's wiring system when you only went in about a new bulb for the cigarette lighter?

However, a vet is very different, for we should be far more emotionally concerned and attached to our dog than we are to our computer or motor car.

So when your vet tells you that your dog has pseudocyesis, don't nod your head seemingly understanding every word only to walk out of the door muttering under your breath. Why not turn around and say "What the heck do you mean?" He will say, "She has a false pregnancy," which is how it should have been explained in the first place.

For after all not all of us have studied Latin or been to veterinary college and it is the job of a good vet or any other good professional to explain clearly and in plain English, although it must be pointed out in fairness that often such complex words are used because there is no standard English alternative.

Most of us feel intimidated by the likes of doctors, solicitors and vets but this should not be the case as in the final analysis you are the customer who is paying for his services. Without you, the vet or any other professional would simply not have a job. So rather than shrinking in the corner when he says "Did you know canine blood consists of 0.8 to 1.0 g/L of glucose?", say to him, "No, I didn't know that. Did you know that the longest moustache ever recorded was 9 feet 2½ inches long?" This will either endear him to you or make him an enemy for life!

There is of course the other type of vet who says almost nothing other than, "Here are the tablets. See you in a week if the dog is no better" at which point you humbly walk out of the door, none the wiser as to your dog's condition.

In these circumstances do feel free to ask such questions as, "What is wrong with my dog?" Ask also if the symptoms are likely to get worse, if the problem could recur, if this illness could lead to anything more serious in the future and, most importantly, how should you care for your dog.

If the vet is not prepared to explain, maybe it is time to make a move to another eminent physician.

But to get a good user-friendly vet is a two way street in that it requires the client to be as thoughtful and helpful as possible. When explaining your dog's symptoms, be precise and to the point, try not to wander into areas that would not be of interest to the vet, such as you were having tea and cakes last Sunday afternoon, which was incidentally a lovely sunny day, with your aunt and whilst discussing how well your flowers had bloomed that year, Jason, your Collie-cross, whilst chasing the ball, got stung by a bee. The only points your vet needs to know are that your dog was stung by a bee, when it happened and symptoms that have occurred since, in order to make a speedy and effective diagnosis. Please afford the same courtesy to the receptionist or veterinary nurse as she may be rushed off her feet that day and not feel well disposed to chit-chat.

Perhaps it is even more important to be clear and precise when asking your vet to make a house-call. The amount of equipment that can be brought to you is limited, so the more details of injury or symptoms that can be given, the greater chance your vet has of bringing the correct equipment and drugs or suggesting that admittance to the surgery is essential, thus not wasting valuable time.

After all, if he turns up

A SOUND EAR. You should clean and inspect your dog's ears regularly. A veterinarian will also check your dog's ears upon each visit to ensure that they are free from mites and infection. Photo by K. Taylor.

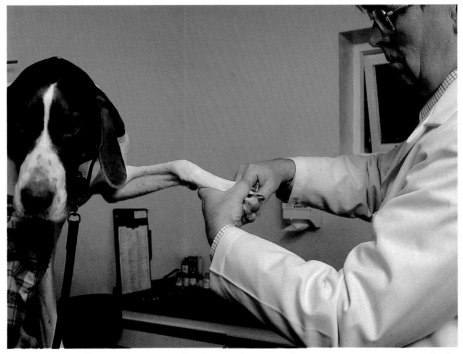

A QUICK REVIEW. Ask your veterinarian to show you the proper way to cut your dog's nails. Photo by R. Hutchings.

expecting to heal a dog with a broken leg only to find it is in a state of unconsciousness, he may be inadequately equipped to help. This is perhaps an opportunity to thank veterinarians for the wonderful work they do and perhaps if your vet has helped you and your dog through a bad time, a thank-you letter wouldn't go amiss. After all, we all like to be appreciated.

A DOCTOR'S VIEW OF THE VETERINARIAN'S WORK

There has been an evident change over recent years in the attitude of veterinarians towards their role and they now take more interest in the well being of the client's family as well as the veterinary needs. Surveys suggest their professional competence is seldom questioned, but the clients are more concerned about how they are treated personally, with respect for their feelings and open communication. Just as doctors have extended their "bedside" manner to cover the patient's family, so veterinarians have developed a "petside" manner to help the owners reach decisions and their involvement is perhaps deeper. Doctors will seldom cover the lifetime of their patients from their first inoculation against poliomyelitis and measles to their passing away. But the veterinarian is often involved from the first injection against distemper until, some ten to 15 years later, he gives the last

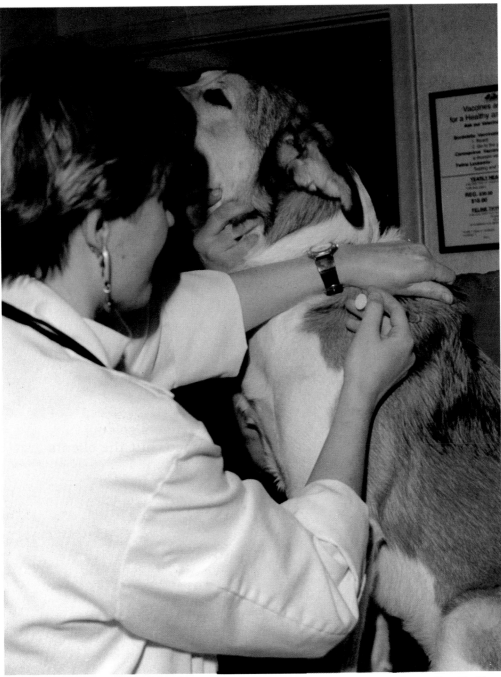

IT'S THAT TIME AGAIN. Yearly inoculations are important in ensuring your dog's good health. Your veterinarian will alert you when it is time for your dog's annual shots. Photo by K. Taylor.

injection.

Both doctors and veterinarians found that as students their training gave them an inadequate education in their future roles as caring professionals, but this is being gradually corrected.

Choosing a First-Class Boarding Kennel

We all want the best for our dogs and try to care for them as well as we can all year 'round. So when holiday time comes around and your dog has to go to a kennel, or perhaps other circumstances make it necessary for your dog to have a stay away from home, selecting accommodations that meet your own standards and pocket may take a little time. A few guidelines should help. There are various types of kennels providing different services including exercise programmes, feeding routines and medical care. Select the kennel that you and your dog like best, for although you make the decision it is always nice to know that your

FIVE-STAR TREATMENT. The kennel you choose should be clean, comfortable and well maintained. Photo by H. Moore.

dog will enjoy his stay there. To find the most suitable type of kennel you may need to look around before making your final choice.

WHERE AND HOW TO FIND YOUR KENNELS

a) Most kennels are listed in the telephone book or any local classified telephone directory.

b) The Environmental Health Department at each local council keeps a list of all kennels in its particular area plus the number of dogs for which each kennel is licensed, the latter information can be very useful if you prefer a smaller, more personal kennel.

c) Although veterinarians keep a list of kennels in their area, they usually do not specifically recommend, unless there is a dog with a complicated medical history that needs special care and attention that a particular kennel can provide.

d) Recommendations from other pet owners are usually a good source of information.

e) Pet shops are another reliable source regarding good local boarding facilities.

f) Dog training clubs are also much aware of which establishments are up to standard.

g) In some countries there is also a publication called "The Kennel Guide" and in the United States, The American Boarding Kennels Association advises and makes reservations.

When you have sorted out your information and decided which kennels to visit, make a list of them and telephone them for an appointment. Do not just turn up. Remember that a kennel is for dogs and the dogs should have priority, not the humans. Time schedules are very tight in most kennels and the manager might not be available or the staff might be busy grooming or feeding the dogs if your arrival is unexpected.

The security aspect for humans and dogs is also high priority on the boarding kennel's agenda; unidentified people, with or without dogs, should report to the kennel's reception area.

Some quarantine and boarding kennels have special visiting hours and it is fairer to everyone if you stick to these.

When you have made your phone calls and are happy with your selection, delete from your list the boarding kennels that do not insist upon up-to-date vaccinations nor recommend immunisation for kennel cough. You should also be allowed to visit their premises and see the actual kennel units where the dogs are kept. If this is not possible discard these establishments also.

Your next step is to visit the boarding kennels that you have selected. You should think of this as a good-will visit in your dog's best interest rather than a major inspection. You are there to look around and receive some useful information. Here are some useful points to bear in mind during your appraisal but remember, in the

HAPPY HOLIDAY. If you are confident that you have left your dog in good hands, you will be able to enjoy your holiday all the more. Photo by H. Moore.

end, it is the same when considering a hotel. If you like the atmosphere, the premises and the owner, then you will probably make the reservation.

When you approach the kennel, ask yourself if the kennel building looks inviting, well maintained and gives a good impression?

Whilst in the kennel building you should see if the premises are light, neat and tidy and smell fresh. Are there good facilities for heating and ventilation? Is the layout practical and welcoming? Are the colours light and soft, for it is commonly known that pale colours are more soothing and comfortable for dogs.

Take a good look at the resident dogs. They should look relaxed, happy and well groomed.

Are you happy with the service and help given by the manager and staff, and, most importantly, would you be happy leaving your dog in their care?

A current kennel license should be correctly displayed in the reception or similar area. You should ask if the kennel has regular veterinary supervision and if there is a vet on call. You may also like to ask if the dogs are taken out for walks, handled and talked to by staff. Usually kennels allow you to bring your dog's toys and bedding. These familiar items can be of great comfort, but it is wise to confirm that this is O.K. before you board your dog.

THE PRICE OF BOARDING

Find out if the cost includes any part of any day, in other words if you deliver your dog at 9 a.m. or 4 p.m. will you still pay the same? Some kennels charge a daily rate after 12 noon, on a similar basis as hotels. It is also worthwhile to ask if the daily rate is inclusive or exclusive of local and government taxes. Some kennels may confirm your booking in writing, whilst others will only do so verbally.

BOOKING IN YOUR DOG

Try to plan ahead and book your dog in as early as possible, remember that good kennels are fully booked (especially during school holidays), sometimes as much as six months to a year in advance.

It is always good to bring your dog in the morning to his holiday kennel so that he can familiarise himself with the new routine and surroundings before "lights out".

When you have delivered your dog it is common practice for the owner to sign an agreement, and furnish the kennels with details such as name, address and telephone number (home and holiday), together with a contact number in case of emergency (which could be a relative or friend who knows your dog very well and can make decisions on your behalf).

Other necessary information is the name, age, sex and breed of dog, your dog's medical history, if relevant, your dog's veterinarian and if your dog has any special diet requirements. Do not forget to take your dog's vaccination record to include the latest date of vaccination and kennel cough immunisation details.

Now your dog's holiday arrangements are complete. You can start to enjoy preparations for your own vacation. Whilst away, if you wish to telephone the boarding kennel to find out how your dog is enjoying his stay, do so, but obviously not too often. After your holiday, when you collect your dog, he should be in as good shape and spirit as when he was delivered, perhaps even better. Naturally, if there has been a medical problem this should have been dealt with by the staff at the kennel or the veterinarian in charge.

As long as both you and your dog had a good holiday, this is what matters, you can then look forward to the next one with peace of mind.

Facing page: AN EXAMPLE OF A BOARDING CONTRACT. Courtesy of Orange Court Kennels.

BOARDING CONTRACT:

BOARDING DETAILS:

Owner _____ Name of Dog _____

Address _____ Telephone Number _____

Emergency Contact:

Name _____ Telephone Number _____

Address _____ **Is your dog insured? Yes/No**

Breed of Dog _____ Sex _____ Date of Birth _____

Period of Boarding from _____ to _____

Collection Time _____ Fee per Boarding Day _____
(Any part of any day)

Bathing, Stripping, Trimming & Grooming Requirements _____

CONDITIONS:

1. A dog accepted for boarding must have been inoculated or booster injected against Distemper, Hepatitis, Leptospirosis and Parvovirus. Certificate must be produced confirming inoculations within the last twelve months. Immunisation against Canine Cough preferred but not essential.

2. Should the dog be taken ill, as determined by the proprietor, the customer's own Veterinary Surgeon will be contacted except in the case of an emergency or where the owner's Veterinary Surgeon is unavailable. The kennel's own Veterinary Surgeon will be called to prescribe any treatment necessary. All fees incurred will be the responsibility of the owner.

   2a. Should the proprietor require any details or medical records from my Veterinary Surgeon, I give my full permission for all information/details to be supplied upon request.

3. Although every care and attention is given all dogs are boarded entirely at the owner's risk and without any liability on the part of the proprietor. The proprietor will not be responsible for the death or loss of any dog left for boarding and will accept any elderly or ill dog at their discretion but totally at the owner's risk.

4. If a dog is left more than two weeks after the agreed collection date without notification from its owner, the proprietor reserves the right to charge a pro rata per day of £6.50 within a period of fourteen days beyond the booking date. If no instructions have been received from the owner by that time, other arrangements will be made to remove the dog from the kennels.

5. Dogs can only be collected/delivered during the following times:
   Monday—Saturday: 10am-12 Noon and 4 pm-6pm   Sunday: 10am-12 noon only.

6. Please telephone or write if you wish to collect your pet before or after the date stated above as the collection date. If the owner advises the proprietor that he wishes to collect the dog prior to the collection date, then all agreed charges will continue to be payable by the owner to the proprietor not withstanding the earlier collection of the dog until the collection date.

7. **Price per boarding day includes any part of any day.**

8. I agree to the above conditions:

Signed _____ Date _____

You may rest assured, that your pet will receive the same loving care and attention that he/she receives at home.

Choosing the Best in Grooming

TOP AND TAIL CARE

By Inger Chapman

It is of course so important that your dog is healthy, fit, comfortable and looks good. A well-looked-after dog is a reflection upon you. One contributing factor to this is the grooming and beauty care of your dog, which can be hard work, but is a necessity for your dog's health and general well being. Even here the saying applies, "prevention is better than cure."

Before you consider buying a particular breed make sure that you fully understand what type of grooming and general care it requires. In the end the two most important factors are time and money—your time and money that you can afford to spend on your dog from puppyhood to adulthood.

The top and tail care consists of: bathing, conditioning, drying (which is optional), ear and eye cleaning, nail cutting, brushing and combing, clipping or stripping. The latter is usually done by a professional canine beautician.

Should you wish to have your dog professionally groomed,

SHAMPOO AND SET. Cleanliness is important for your dog's good health and general well being. If you do not have the time to groom your dog yourself, find a reputable canine beautician to do the job for you. Photo by I. Francais.

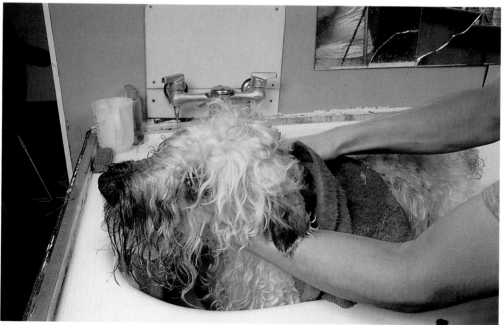

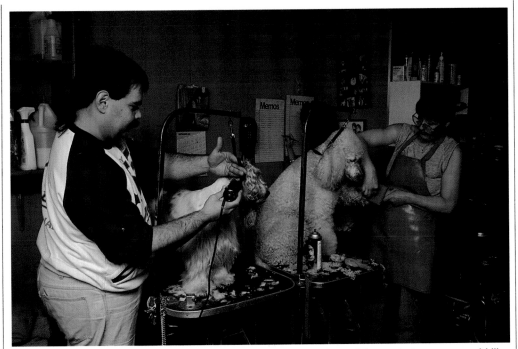

WASH AND BRUSH UP. Make sure you instruct your canine beautician as to how you would like your dog to be styled. Photo by I. Francais.

clipped and bathed, make sure you go to a reputable, licensed establishment with a qualified staff. Usually each beauty parlour has its own particular style and "speciality" breeds. Before you leave your dog, do make sure you have told the canine beautician which style you would like your dog to have (we expect all women who go to the hairdressers will appreciate the importance of this, and perhaps some men have had an unexpected hair cut!). It is also a good idea to mention if your dog has a behavioural problem, such as being fidgety or snappy. This will help and prepare the beautician before starting her task.

D.I.Y. GROOMING

Remember that if you have accustomed your puppy to grooming sessions from a very early age by handling him all over with a little grooming, this will make life a lot easier when dealing with the older dog.

If you are a first-time dog owner and want to do grooming and clipping yourself, ask your dog's breeder and your breed society for help, but most importantly start gradually, especially if you have a dog that needs to be clipped in a certain way according to a breed standard.

Grooming can vary upon the actual breed and coat of the dog. Brushing and combing can easily be done by the owner. It is also a wonderful therapy for both dog and owner and should be done in a relaxed atmosphere. The handling of the dog should always be firm but gentle.

Grooming must start early and the puppy must learn to sit or stand still while getting used to the feel of the brush strokes, which can sometimes be ticklish and soothing so the dog will certainly react accordingly.

If you have a small breed of dog, make sure you put him on a raised surface (such as an old table covered with a clean bath/car mat), making sure he is safe and cannot fall or slip. This is to ensure that you can brush your dog comfortably and reach your dog's less accessible areas with the brush. At the same time check him over for any foreign particles, for example, ticks, grass seeds, burrs. Remember, don't grovel on the floor with your dog, stand up high and make him behave—you are in charge (hopefully!).

There are various breeds with different types of coats and some with no hair at all such as the Mexican Hairless and the Chinese Crested (who have a little hair around the face and tail).

There are wire-haired breeds such as terriers, long-haired such as the Old English Sheepdog and Tibetan Terrier, short-haired such as the Siberian Husky and Elkhound, smooth-coated such as the Pointers and Dobermanns, curly-coated such as the Curly Coated Retriever and Portuguese Water Dog, and corded-coated as in the Hungarian Puli and Komondor.

It goes without saying that the long-haired and wire-haired breeds are difficult to groom and maintain regularly, which should be borne in mind before you buy your puppy. Another important point to consider is human allergies to dogs, naturally long-haired and wire-haired dogs are more likely to cause an allergy than a smooth-coated dog.

As a general rule long-haired breed puppies look gorgeous, but be aware they do grow up and have a very difficult coat to brush and maintain.

Shopping List For Grooming Short-coated Breeds

1) Brush—boar bristle, soft, medium, stiff.

2) Comb—medium-sized teeth to remove deep hairs.

3) Slicker—brush to remove old hairs.

4) Scissors—for ordinary thinning.

Shopping List for Grooming Long-haired Breeds

1) Brush—Boar bristle, stiff.

2) Comb—large, extra long teeth.

3) Specially designed slicker brush.

4) Rake—for de-tangling coat.

5) Scissors—for ordinary thinning.

Shopping List for Grooming Smooth-coated Breeds

1) Horsehair brush (glove brush)—for polishing coat.

2) Rubber glove—for removing loose hairs.

3) Chamois leather—for polishing coat.

This list is an example of items available for the basic grooming of pet dogs.

TEETH

Nowadays quite a few people brush their dog's teeth. This has become more important with the advent of complete dog foods and soft foods which do not massage and clean as effectively as diets years ago. Special toothpastes and brushes are available from your veterinarian and pet shop or perhaps you prefer to use one of your old brushes. In addition there are Nylabone® products that have a cleaning action for your dog's teeth and also massage the gums.

FEET CARE

You should regularly check your dog's feet between the pads for grass seeds, burrs, etc., even if your dog is regularly clipped and checked over by a canine beautician.

NAIL CARE

Nails and dewclaws should also be checked on a regular basis although most breeds have their dewclaws removed when they are puppies. Even better still, some breeds are born without them. Some dogs' nails grow very fast and need to be clipped, while others are worn down by exercise on a hard surface. There are three types of nail clippers: the scissor type, the guillotine type and the pliers type. The first two types are suitable for small to medium-sized breeds, the latter for large breeds. It is, however, an individual preference which type is, or feels, best to use. Nail clippers can be bought in well-stocked pet shops, veterinary surgery shops, canine mail order

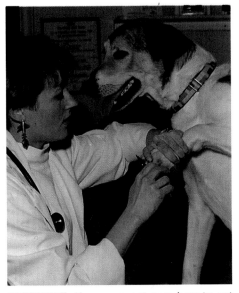

PETICURE. If you are not sure how to cut your dog's nails safely, let your canine beautician or veterinarian do it. Photo by K. Taylor.

catalogues and trade stand exhibitions. Large championship shows will also have stands that sell grooming equipment.

The main thing is to cut your dog's nails accurately and painlessly. If you are worried and feel unsure of this task, don't do it. Let a canine beautician or your veterinarian do it. Perhaps when you feel more confident you can cut your dog's nails under supervision. It is better to consult a professional than cut the quick by mistake, which causes bleeding, upsetting to both owner and dog. In case this does happen, the bleeding will stop after a while but a coagulant powder can be used to stop the bleeding instantly.

EARS

All breeds should have their ears checked on a weekly basis to avoid ear infections, mites, etc.

Breeds with long ears such as Cocker Spaniels, Poodles and Old English Sheepdogs, should have most of their hair cut or removed from the inner side of the ear so that the air can flow freely into the ear canal. This is a job which should be done by professionals.

Breeds with pointed ears, such as German Shepherd Dogs, Corgis and West Highland White Terriers, should still be checked regularly and cleaned.

The cleaning of the ear can be done with a piece of cotton wool dampened with baby oil or an appropriate ear cleaner. Make sure that you handle the dog gently but firmly, giving him a titbit if he is being very good so he will associate the ear cleaning with something beneficial.

There are quite a few medicated powders on the market, but they must be used very sparingly, even better not used at all because they can cause blockage in the inner ear.

The inside must not be touched but you must check the ear for large amounts of wax or smelly, brown-coloured discharge. Ear infections can be serious and should be treated by a veterinarian.

EYE CARE

Your dog's eye care is very important. Obviously such breeds as Cavalier King Charles Spaniels, Pekingese, Pugs, Bulldogs and King Charles Spaniels are breeds with protruding eyes and wrinkles, which need to be

WISE EYES. The Cavalier King Charles Spaniel has large, round eyes that need special care and attention, more than most other breeds. Photo by Z. Skivington.

checked more regularly than other breeds. Eyes are fairly easy to check and clean; always use a *clean* damp cotton wool ball or a cold used tea bag with movements away from the eyes. Should the eyes look red, sore or have a yellow discharge, contact your veterinarian.

CANINE BATH CARE

Your shopping list for your dog's bathing items should be as follows:

Canine shampoo, canine conditioner, baby shampoo, brush, comb, bath mat, two good-sized towels.

There are various ways of wetting your dog (and yourself!), such as using a hose in the bath, shower base, or outside using a hose pipe. Put a nylon collar on your dog and if your dog is determined to escape your clutches, attach the collar to a lead and secure him to a fixed point or enlist help. The collar and lead should not discolour and should give half a metre slack.

Make sure you use *lukewarm* water, never hot, and wet the coat thoroughly before applying shampoo. This should be massaged in. Remember to put baby shampoo on your dog's head.

Whilst your dog is in the bath it is a good idea to check his ears and clean them with a damp face flannel. For the best result put the shampoo on twice and thereafter the conditioner. Whilst the conditioner is on brush or comb through the coat then rinse thoroughly.

Strictly speaking, conditioner should not be applied to Poodles or terriers as owners prefer these dogs not to have a "soft" coat.

USEFUL HINTS

Always brush your dog before bathing him to remove dead hairs and allow shampoo and water to penetrate properly.

Always put a bath mat down and disinfect afterwards.

Always use baby shampoo on your dog's head—this is much kinder to his eyes. If you have to use a medicated shampoo put some petroleum jelly around your dog's eyes, taking care when shampooing and rinsing. If you have run out of dog shampoo use a mild shampoo, such as a baby product.

Make sure you have the correct equipment on hand before you start to groom your dog.

Remember you can pass on your mood and anxiety to your dog so be calm, gentle and firm, then both of you will enjoy it.

If you live near the coast, remember that sea water is good for the skin, but is not good for the coat so rinse your dog after he has had a dip.

If you have bathed a light-coloured or white dog, never put a red leather collar on a wet coat. It discolours immediately, necessitating a repeat bath.

The Genetic Framework

A dog's mind, when it is born, is rather like an empty bookcase.

Although some dogs seem to come with it half filled:

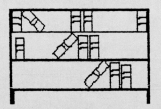

You can allow it to fill with a collection of irrelevant information:

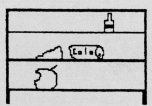

Or guide your dog to a full, useful and uncluttered mind.

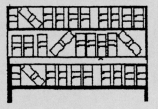

A DIAMOND IN THE ROUGH. All puppies are capable of being trained, although some take longer than others. An owner should be exceptionally gentle and patient during puppy training. Photo by I. Francais.

A Little Love and Understanding

THE DRIVE AND THE MOTIVATION

Our dogs' main motivations are those of sex (the giver of life), food (the sustainer of life) and love (the love of those who care for our lives). The order in which an individual dog is motivated and the degree to which each element drives the individual, to a large extent, will determine their overall personality. Food, however, is the main motivator with a majority of dogs. This is naturally understandable as the instinct for survival will necessitate this drive. We find that many puppies who have been extremely well cared for

THE GOLDEN RETRIEVER loves the water almost as much as he does his master and home. Photo by P. Williams.

from birth and have not been fed from the "communal bowl" are far less motivated in this respect than the dog who, from the litter, has had to ensure its quota by fair means or foul. This early conditioning will affect the dog throughout his life, for despite the fact that their food is now amply and regularly supplied, their behaviour pattern in the first six weeks of life has been so deeply implanted that change is unlikely, or difficult, to say the least.

A German Shepherd Dog, Kim, had been wandering the streets of Brighton for some time before being rescued. He naturally became a scavenger and despite going to his next owner, an elderly lady who supplied him with constant gourmet dog food, the habit still remained deeply implanted to find food when and where he could and to take any opportunity to fill up his tummy.

Owners often find when they have one dog who is a placid or even picky eater that by introducing another dog into the household who may devour food voraciously, the original dog would become much quicker when eating and far more protective over its food. It may be assumed that it perceives the second dog as a competitor for its food.

Because the male dog's metabolic rate will slow down considerably after castration, owners and veterinary surgeons alike are concerned that the dog will put on weight. It is regrettable that, despite advice to cut down on the dog's intake of food, another strange phenomenon occurs. Dogs who were highly sexually motivated, which is presumably the reason for their castration in the first place, may suddenly switch their prime motivator to that of food, compounding the problem of keeping our dogs in shape. A dog may have high sexual motivation that may manifest itself in behavioural problems, such as escaping, running off or tracking in search of his favourite pursuit—sex, clearly necessitating the need to remove the problem at its source.

Whilst the dog who is motivated by its love of humans can be a joy to its owner, problems may occur when motivation levels are too high. For example, dogs that are so predisposed often have severe anxiety problems when left, even for short periods of time, others may be so in love with the human race in general that they go up to every passing stranger craving attention. (It is a very interesting phenomenon that dogs normally do not display high motivation levels in more than one category and when such a category is removed they may switch to another prime motivator.)

The genetically motivated dog may not of course fit into any of these motivation categories. Examples are:

The Border Collie who has an inherent drive to round up or chase.

THE ENGLISH SPRINGER SPANIEL is noted for its excellent nose and hunting abilities. Photo by A. Chen.

The Lurcher who may have an extraordinary desire to hunt.

The Springer Spaniel who sniffs constantly at the ground using his searching abilities.

The German Shepherd Dog with his extreme levels of protective behaviour.

The retriever with a deep and passionate love of water sports.

In conclusion, knowing something about your dog's motivation (personality) will help you considerably when selecting your puppy, when training and when seeking help for behavioural problems.

Food in Training

NECESSITY/OBSESSION/HELP OR HINDRANCE

Should we use food in order to motivate our dogs to behave? Certainly such motivational stimulation can induce spectacular short-term training results, but will the effect be lasting or will we simply end up with an overweight, uncontrollable dog?

This section will attempt to answer this question about the most controversial aspect of modern training techniques. For example, with a titbit in your hand and the dog aware of it, raise your arm from waist to shoulder height. This is almost guaranteed to make your dog sit. Now with some dogs, this exercise constantly repeated will condition them to respond to such a hand signal, even when they have been weaned off titbits for training purposes.

However, the hungry dog will soon be motivated to move towards you, a result which is not desired in this particular exercise, whilst the greedy dog will probably leap at your hand expecting a food reward. A dramatic example of this occurred when a Dobermann, belonging to a lady in Kent, injured its owner's hand in a frenzied belief that food was forthcoming, having come to expect this through food-conditioning training. This may be a particularly profound example, but using food as a motivator for some dogs causes them to go into a state of uncontrollable excitement.

Training of this type has also been shown to have poor long-term results. A dog so encouraged in its early life may soon resent the fact that food rewards are no longer given, the best results from such methods being often seen in dogs who would have responded under almost any training philosophy.

Imagine your young child throws tantrums going into school. You offer your child a bar of chocolate if he goes in and presto—your child obeys. But what happens on the next day? Will he want two bars? Surely all this child is learning is that the more fuss he makes, the greater the reward.

What about the day you leave the chocolate at home?

Such similarities can be readily drawn with dogs who have been taught to recall through food motivation. In essence the food is being used to replace an inherent desire, say to run off and play with another dog, with a stronger desire (that of food). But if food is the lesser desire than playing with the other dog, then we will surely lose, resulting in a negative response from the dog. This of course is particularly true of the dog who may have just eaten dinner, be off his food perhaps because of hot weather, or simply not be a highly food-motivated individual.

IS THERE A TIME AND PLACE FOR FOOD MOTIVATIONAL TRAINING?

Yes, we can often use food when encouraging our dogs to perform exercises other than those required for day-to-day living (walking to heel and recall, etc.). Very often food is used in the early stages of agility training where a dog may feel unsure at scaling the A-frame, going through the tunnel and over the dog walk or even to encourage such extraordinary feats as jumping through hoops of fire.

FOOD: THE POSITIVE EFFECTS FOR BEHAVIOUR MODIFICATION

A dog who reacts aggressively to oncoming humans may be successfully re-educated by the use of food. For example, Oscar, a two-year-old mongrel, would growl and bite any hand suddenly coming towards his face. Continual use of food offered by numerous, but specified, strangers modified his perception and the seemingly oncoming threat was later to become a friendly advance.

ALL FIRED UP! Dog jumping through a hoop of fire. Photo by T. Buckley.

The Hand-Shy Dog

Typically the dog who has been rescued and may have been treated badly by its previous owner, especially if the dog has been hit, may exhibit a nervous reaction when a hand is raised. In order to reduce such a reaction, food may be put into the bowl by hand as with the dog who is aggressive with food; but in this instance, over a period of time, the hand is raised higher and higher and dropped suddenly to the bowl. This can also be used on any occasion where a titbit may be given and, if possible, enlisting helpers to do the same.

Training—The Controversy

THE DESIRE/COMPULSION RATIO

Note: For the academics amongst our readers, such as psychologists, psychiatrists and zoologists, a more suitable heading for this chapter may have been the familiar "Approach/Avoid Conflict", however, the purpose of this book is to make the easiest possible reading for the 'lay' dog owner.

Why is it that some books we read on training seem to contradict others completely? Why do we get conflicting opinions from club instructors, professional trainers and behaviourists?

There are many methods and approaches to training. This does not mean that one is right or one is wrong. To quote Barry Linford, Senior Course Instructor, Obedience Division of the British Institute of Professional Dog Trainers, "If it is kind and it works, use it".

Irrespective of approach, however, we feel the necessity to explain the differences: why one thing works for one dog and a completely different approach works for another and analyse questions such as "Do you bribe your dog with food?" or "Do you put a check chain around its neck?"

By understanding a little about our dog's mind we can

better understand what we are doing and why we are doing it, appreciating the differences between each dog's personality (even within a breed) and enjoying their individual characters that make them so endearing to humans.

Dogs are not robots. They have their own personalities, their own motivations and are as individual as we are.

THE EXPLANATION

In order to control a particular behavioural problem it is necessary to understand the desire/compulsion ratio factor. (The word compulsion is commonly used by dog trainers although aversion or deterrent may be a better term.)

On the one hand the dog may have an inherent desire to indulge in a certain behavioural pattern. Some examples are: running off, pulling on the lead, acting aggressively towards other dogs. This behaviour may have been induced through the dog's social environment and experiences from birth or it may be part of the dog's genetic structure (hereditary) or can be part of the dog's physiological condition. In order to correct this behaviour, a sufficient degree of compulsion must be applied to modify the dog's behavioural programming. If only we could explain to our dog "the error of its ways" or sit the dog down in front of a training video! This is regrettably impossible as this is not the way dogs' minds work. Let's compare the delinquent dog's thoughts to those of a bank robber. The compulsion for stopping this person from re-offending may well be the thought of getting 20 years in jail. This creates a balance in his mind, his desire to re-offend is balanced out by the compulsion (jail sentence). Let's assume the law was changed and the sentence for such offences was reduced to two days in prison. This would cause the scales to be out of balance and in this situation we suspect it would encourage the criminal to re-offend.

This is not unlike canine behaviour. When raiding the larder the dog obsessed with food would not be deterred by an insipid command of "Leave that alone, Bonzo darling". Surely in this instance the desire would outweigh the compulsion. The remedy, therefore, is to find a suitable deterrent level needed to stop this behaviour (assuming that the dog has been adequately fed), while always adopting the kindest approach.

Recall can impose the ultimate dilemma with our dogs. Suppose the bank robber knows that his getaway car is twice as fast as any police car. The knowledge will dilute the level of restraint (compulsion) as his chances of being caught are reduced. Dogs have an even better advantage as the chances of chastising them when they are running at 20 miles an hour are impossible, even for the Olympic runner!

Some dogs would respond to recall training in a club hall, but then be completely disobedient outside. The missing factor is a high desire level. In this restricted environment the dog cannot escape and environmental stimulation is limited. With the dog in the field the desire level soars and the compulsion level may need to be increased.

Food training offers a similar dilemma. What we are trying to do here is to replace one desire with a stronger one. Look at it from your dog's point of view: Would you rather be running around a field in delight or receiving a couple of doggy choc drops and being taken home? The filled-up tummy syndrome also comes into play as the sated dog will have a lower desire level for food. On the other hand some dog's desire for food is so great that under the same circumstances the scales would be tipped to a positive position and induce a fine recall.

If food is not a prime motivator for your dog and the recall problems get seriously out of hand, a last resort may be that the trainer would decide to use a radio-controlled collar, which would induce a *mild* electric shock to reinforce the owner's command. This should not be considered cruel as the bottom line for this dog may be that he gets run over or shot by an irate farmer. In this instance a strong compulsion is being employed to balance the scales of a strong desire.

THE OTHER SIDE OF THE SCALE

One of the most common problems owners face is when their puppy starts to cut its teeth. In this situation the dog has an extraordinarily high desire to chew in order to alleviate considerable pain. All the compulsion in the world will not stop your dog chewing and even a smack would be construed as unkind in these circumstances.

This type of problem is tackled in an entirely different way. We now redress the balance of our scales by reducing the dog's desire, in this case simply by reducing the element of pain as far as possible with pain killers from your veterinarian.

The dog who is running off into danger because of sexual desire should similarly not be unduly reprimanded for such an uncontrollable feeling. It must surely be better to reduce the desire therefore necessitating a lower, or nil, compulsion level.

The lonely dog who chews up the furniture because he is left for 12 hours a day should not be held to blame. Left for only a short time he would be most unlikely to exhibit such behaviour. We are therefore in a position to reduce the desire level and stop the problem.

Reduction of the desire level may be likened to the bank robber who has just won a million dollars. This good fortune clearly reduces his desire level to commit a crime!

Behaviourists and trainers

should therefore be thinking about the reduction in desire levels rather than the increase in compulsion.

Surely there can be no greater pleasure than training a dog with mild or almost no compulsion at all, simple repetitive work sufficing. Check chains and other compulsive methods will prove unnecessary and both owner and dog are happy from day one. This must be the ideal relationship and it is the case with the vast majority of dogs. Indeed, many dogs seem to be born with all the "nice ways" and what a delight they are.

Humans and dogs both receive two distinct types of behavioural motivation from the brain, referred to as "emotionally stimulated behaviour" and "reason-stimulated behaviour".

Children up to the ages of three or four years respond mentally very much as dogs do, but after this age humans tend to develop their reasoning abilities and change their behavioural motivation. Up to the age of four, much of what humans learn is based on the simple pain/pleasure syndrome, although the word "pain" may be too emotive in this respect. An unhappy or uncomfortable association at an early age may well cause a lifelong aversion to the source. I remember as a child being taken to the hospital with suspected meningitis. My mother gave me mushroom soup before the ambulance arrived.

This caused me to dislike mushroom soup intensely for the next ten years, although I am happy to say that all turned out well and mushroom soup is back on the menu.

Similarly the dog brought home from the breeder in an overheated car on a four-hour journey may produce a permanent car-sickness problem and a dislike of travelling.

However, this very association may also be employed to the owner's benefit to modify undesirable behavioural patterns such as inducing sickness to stop a dog from eating faeces.

THE REASON-BLOCKING MECHANISM

Humans may have the "edge" in terms of our perception of intelligence due to our higher reasoning levels; however, our ability to reason also blocks our ability to learn quickly and without question. So on the plus side a dog will learn at a much quicker rate than its human counterpart because, unlike a child, a dog questions the commands he is given far less. Humans tend to debate and argue (outwardly or subliminally) from an early age, slowing down their response to their peers. If your dog did the same, it might take 18 years to train.

Let's take a profound example of this phenomena. Not so long ago, electrodes were attached to people who wished to give up smoking. On lighting up a cigarette, the smoker received an electric shock. The idea of such therapy was that the recipient associated the act of lighting up or inhaling a cigarette with pain. This method failed dramatically because the smoker went home, reasoned that no wires were attached to him now, craved a cigarette and deduced that it was now safe to light up! It is very fortunate that our dogs do not make such deductions. If our dogs were able to smoke, such therapy would most likely work with them. Of course, one must conclude that dogs would not be silly enough to smoke! By the same token, a human may be persuaded to give up the habit, a course of action not available to successfully re-educate a dog.

We hope this will in some way explain why such obnoxious devices such as check chains and electric collars are used on our dogs. Perhaps when our understanding becomes greater and our dogs evolve further such things may be thrown away. We look forward to that day.

AREA/CIRCUMSTANCE CONDITIONING

It becomes apparent when watching some dogs drag their owners out of training school and along the road as if no training had ever been undertaken, that something has gone sadly wrong.

It may simply be that having done their stint, the owner no

OUTDOOR TRAINING. If you and your dog attend obedience classes, suggest that the instructor conduct some classes outside, weather permitting, to avoid area conditioning. Photo by A. Mozol.

ON THE BEACH. Maintain your own training programme in places where you would normally take your dog for exercise. Acclimating your dog to different areas and circumstances will make him more manageable. Photo by A. Campbell.

longer sees the necessity to maintain an equal level of discipline. More likely the dog has been *area-conditioned*, associating training with a particular area or circumstance. The answer is to change training venues regularly, encourage your club to use outdoor facilities in the better weather and maintain your own training programme in public areas where you would normally take your dog. Do expect the possibility of an audience!

This phenomenon is equally true when considering *circumstance conditioning*. How often will the perfectly trained town dog be suddenly, totally out of control in the country environment, stimulated by the open spaces, wildlife and farm animals. Conversely the country dog may similarly go to pieces when placed in a bustling town environment.

In conclusion the more areas and circumstances that have been encountered during your dog's learning and training process, the more likely it will be that your dog's behaviour will be stable in a variety of situations.

"Can it be kind to be cruel?" We believe the answer can be "yes" but, unlike some cruel teachers of yesteryear or aggressive parents, we must never abuse our privilege as masters.

Association and Memory

Why shouldn't I scold my dog when after spending an hour trying to get him back he wanders up, tail wagging, without a care in the world, having made me late for work? Dog owners are often most perplexed by the subject of when to, and when not to, scold a dog.

The first confusion arises out of the misconception that dogs only have a short memory. They do not. A dog's memory is for life. The much loved Golden Retriever, Hustler, being an extremely well-balanced and well-trained chap, had one little quirk. When he was six months old, the poor soul's tail got accidentally caught in a shop's heavy swing-glass door. Fortunately no physical damage occurred but forever after he would walk past the shop intently watching the door and wrapping himself around his owner's legs showing signs of considerable distress. It would have been tantamount to impossible to get him into the shop, short of carrying him.

Dogs, however, do have a very limited level of association. Let's put it this way, if your child had taken some cookies from the jar without asking, even if this misdemeanour had not been spotted until the next day, a telling off would still induce an association level, one high enough for the child to remember and for

it to be effective. Additionally, your child may have done exceptionally well in an examination at school and the fact that praise was received some time later does not diminish the effect. Conversely, a doggy treat after a successful training session would not render any useful association in your dog's memory bank.

Clearly the bonus of language and the higher reasoning abilities come into play, but even so the route to the brain is still very different with the human and canine processes.

Our dogs have a very limited association span. Research has shown this to be as little as three seconds in duration. Why should it be any longer? They simply need to react instantly to given situations for protection and survival. So when our dog returns after an hour of frustrated calling he will need to be encouraged and praised in order that the act of returning is associated with a pleasurable experience. The same rules apply when we wish to correct such behaviour; discipline (compulsion) needs to be instant—catching the dog in the act. This is difficult when a dog is prancing around at 20 miles an hour, but by using the "lobbing check chain" or the electric collar such behaviour can readily be corrected.

In other words we have given

MEMORIES. Although a dog's memory is long, his association span is quite limited. Photo by T.B. Chadwick.

instant correction during the act to obtain the correct association.

However such devices as electronic collars in wrong or inexperienced hands may easily lead to an incorrect association in the dog's mind. A dog fighting with another and being given a shock from the electric collar may perceive the other dog as the cause, which would simply heighten the problems.

The German Shepherd Dog, Kim, who took great delight in head-butting other dogs, was corrected by using an electric collar, but only as an enforcement of the owner's commands, always at least six feet from his intended victim.

On one occasion, however, the collar malfunctioned as he was about to pick up his favourite ball. It took three months to fully regain his confidence in that and every other ball—another example of mis-association at its worst.

Equipment

To drill a concrete wall with a hand drill would be considered difficult, uncomfortable and time consuming. Using poor equipment to train your dog may be equally unproductive.

PUPPY EQUIPMENT

Choose a suitable collar for your puppy that allows plenty of room for expansion. Puppies grow exceedingly fast and we would suggest not spending too much on items for the young dog as the equipment will soon become redundant.

An inexpensive nylon puppy lead will suffice. Choose one that is comfortable to your hand and has a good, secure clip.

LEADS/LEASHES

A piece of rope or an old tie would suffice to train your dog, having no effect on the overall success of the training, but comfort and security are the key words here. Particularly the owner of a large, pulling dog would benefit greatly from a comfortable lead. Generally leads are made of nylon, leather or chain with a handle. Whilst nylon leads are perfectly acceptable there is a tendency to chafe the hands. Chain leads, often purchased because a dog is chewing at the lead, can cause considerable discomfort particularly when cold and wet. They have often been the cause of cut hands.

So if your dog is chewing the lead, stop him rather than purchase less suitable equipment. A good-quality bridle leather (or buffalo hide) lead will certainly pay dividends in terms of strength and comfort. Beware of leads made of inferior materials, such as composites and plastics. The leather should be supple and have suitably

TYPES OF HOOKS. *(Left)* scissor or quick release hook; *(middle)* snap hook; *(right)* trigger hook. Illustrations by G. Horn.

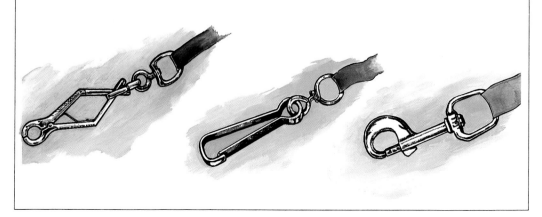

rounded edges. Leads should be of an adequate length, in fact the shorter the dog the more necessary a longer lead is. In general terms a lead of approximately 4 feet is desirable. Should you have two dogs, it may be advantageous to purchase a "double leash", this type has clips on each end.

The hook is of vital importance for the dog's security. Normally, leads are fitted with a trigger hook ideally suited for our purposes. Make sure it is of strong metal, such as brass or steel, and not a cheap alloy as these will tend to break at the most unfortunate moment. Furthermore check the spring action to ensure adequate operation. Scissor hooks or quick-release devices are often used by security and police forces for instant release, but they do have a tendency to release at inopportune moments and are not recommended for the novice owner. Many people buy short leads in order to restrain their dogs but this is not the best method.

SLIP COLLARS AND HALF-CHECK COLLARS

These devices are ideally suited for the dog that does not have a severe pulling tendency. They are much kinder in use as the severity of the checking action is far better controlled, particularly for the over-zealous handler. They are far more desirable for the young, the delicate dog, or small breeds. However, they do not have the same level of compulsion as check chains.

CORRECT FITTING OF A CHECK CHAIN. Illustration by G. Horn.

CHECK CHAIN

The dog who does not adequately respond when using slip and half-check collars will require a full-check chain. The check chain used correctly is an invaluable aid to owners and trainers, but if used incorrectly becomes a potential noose for the dog to hang itself. Dogs suffering from long periods of walking with a tight chain may develop the "wheezy dog syndrome", prevalent with badly handled Labradors. It is the considered opinion of the authors that the proper use of a check chain (sometimes incorrectly referred to as a "choke chain") should be demonstrated by a person qualified or experienced to do so. We do not believe that it can adequately be shown in a book. This may seem odd but we have met so many people who have read "how to use a check chain" and still have not grasped its safe and effective use.

Please understand that the idea of a check chain is to induce a short sharp jerking sensation on the dog's neck coupled with the auditory stimulation he receives as the chain moves. It is most definitely not intended to choke a dog.

WARNING: Check chains and slip collars must be removed before dog's play commences.

HEAD-RESTRAINING COLLARS

Their concept is akin to that of a horse bridle. It works on the principle that if the dog pulls, its head is turned inwards and thus its power to pull is physically limited. Such items can be extremely effective in stopping dogs from pulling, but they tend to moderate the dog's desire to pull rather than inducing a compulsion that will have a greater effect in terms of actual teaching.

It will be advantageous to seek advice when using such an implement. Some dogs have a head formation that hampers the correct fitting of the head restraining collar, which may cause injuries especially to the eyes. Many dogs will demonstrate an intense dislike to these devices and under these circumstances they should not be used. Dogs with inherent neck problems, such as the Dobermann with osteospondylitis, may have their condition worsened by the use of the head restraining collar. It is therefore important to seek veterinary advice if in doubt.

SPIKED COLLAR

This item is widely used on the continent of Europe, although banned in the U.K. It is important to understand the nature of this device as the word "spike" does not define its use. The actual method of operation is that the prongs, which are blunt and are not designed to puncture, come together when the dog pulls and cause the skin to be pinched. The definition therefore of such a device would more correctly be pinch collar.

Can this device be justified? It is the opinion of the authors that such devices may have a very small role to play, an example being of a lady who contracted a rare spine disease making her unable to correct her dog in the normal way. Faced with re-housing her dog, perhaps the pinch collar could be considered the best option.

THE HARNESS

In most cases it is found that the harness actually propagates pulling. Its normal usage is for tracking; however, pulling is encouraged. There is always the exception to the rule, one such being a German Shepherd Dog, Asta, who did not respond to any known correction methods until the harness was employed by her owner for tracking. Although Asta decided she would walk to heel when on the harness, we must stress that this is unusual as pulling would normally be made worse.

LINES AND EXTENDABLE LEADS

Dogs, when on the lead, should be encouraged to walk to heel and then offered the freedom of a run off the lead. We cannot condone dogs being allowed to wander on long lines. If you have a recall problem, for example, solve it rather than allow this "betwixt and between" behaviour. Lines and extendable leads, however, can prove very useful for the practising of recall exercises.

MUZZLES

New dog laws in the U.K. require certain breeds of dogs, such as the Pit Bull Terrier, to be muzzled under a new Act of Parliament known as the Dangerous Dogs Act. Indeed in Republic of Ireland 12 such breeds are defined under this legislation. Where a dog is known to be dangerous one can see no alternative but to use a muzzle and one has no choice within the definition of the Act. But before using such an item under other circumstances, seek advice as to the true nature of your dog's problem as there may be other methods of controlling or curing his undesirable behaviour. These devices will tend to have a catapult effect, often making the dog more aggressive and also putting the dog in an unfair position where it cannot defend itself.

Taking such a device off after aggressive emotions have been heightened can prove dangerous to the owner so great care must be taken when "de-muzzling" a dog.

Any legislation requiring muzzling is unworkable unless a manufacturing standard as to the item's quality and workability is established. Many muzzles can be detrimental to the dog's well being, disliked intensely by the dog resulting in him continually trying to force it off, or simply so badly made as to be unreliable especially in volatile situations.

PERSONAL ATTACK ALARMS AND ULTRA-SONIC DETERRENTS

Separating two dogs who are fighting is exceedingly dangerous and none of us can be sure, however nice the nature of our dogs, that an unexpected attack may never happen. We would encourage all owners who walk their dogs in public areas to take such a device with them in order to separate a fight, or at least to switch the dogs' attention away, giving the owners time to safely separate them.

Dogs displaying aggressive tendencies would become quickly tolerant of such devices, its use therefore is not intended for the regularly attacking dog, but for the unexpected encounter.

ELECTRONIC DEVICES (RADIO-CONTROLLED COLLARS)

In the U.K. the subject of this equipment invites enormous controversy, although perhaps use of such equipment is more widely accepted in other parts of the world.

The authors of this book spent many hours mulling over the possibility of excluding this item from the publication due to its controversial nature, but surely as this equipment becomes more and more widely available this subject must not be conveniently dismissed as would have been an easier option. For such equipment used correctly, with sensitivity, kindness and a good understanding of the dog's problems, and not as an excuse for shoddy training or as a short cut, like other advancements in this technological age, can have its role in behavioural modification.

The whole personality and environmental conditions of the dog should be considered before such training methods are commenced. Having been advised by a suitably qualified trainer or behaviourist that use of such equipment was necessary, you may well like to consider consulting your vet as to whether your dog's personality and physical condition would permit the safest possible use of this item. An appraisal of the dog's future must be considered before poo-pooing the use of electronic collars.

For example, if a dog was worrying sheep would a mild shock from a collar be considered cruel if the alternative was the dog being shot by a farmer? Would a dog who was in the habit of running out of a park into traffic, potentially the cause of a serious traffic incident, be better off being "buzzed" with a collar in order to correct this behavioural problem?

This type of determined dog who defies milder forms of training leaves the conscientious owner with no alternative but to seek expert tuition where the use of such equipment may be advised after all alternative methods have been tried.

Make sure your trainer or behaviourist initially uses such a device in a secure area or on a sturdy line in case the device causes the dog to panic; although this is unlikely, it is a possibility that needs to be considered.

Furthermore, under these controlled conditions an optimum level (preferably the minimum level) may be found, for example, one that produces a response but does not cause trauma.

Careful use of this equipment is paramount. Serious psychological damage could occur with a nervous dog. An aggressive dog who associated the shock as being caused by its adversary (the dog it was attacking) could well respond by stepping up its aggression. If, however, in the same situation the collar was used to reinforce the owner's call to "come" whilst the dog was still at a good distance from its quarry, this would be considered proper use of the collar. These devices therefore may be used as an "extension" to our own arms, enabling us to correct our dogs when they are at a considerable distance and/or going at a great speed.

ANTI-BARKING COLLAR

Barking is very often a symptom of a more deeply underlying problem. Having considered sexual, dietary and environmental factors, perhaps such a device may be necessary. If the barking is in the presence of the owner, a squirt of water from a clean washing-up liquid bottle

BARKING UP THE WRONG TREE? Barking may be a symptom of a more serious problem. Before resorting to anti-barking devices, consider sexual, dietary and environmental factors. Photo by Mrs. H.J. Wilkinson.

accompanied by the command "quiet" can be extremely effective. If this fails or is impractical, the barking collar may prove necessary.

The U.K. situation is delicate, as cheap imports caused the public to perceive these devices to be unkind. It is most likely that had a high-quality American version been used first such controversy would not have reigned. These highly developed collars can prove invaluable training aids to the dog who barks incessantly. As we have said before, such devices using electric-shock methods must only be used subject to the dog's physical and emotional stability and again, if in doubt, consult your veterinarian.

So perhaps you may prefer to consider the next item as a kinder method of dealing with barking:

THE OLFACTORY COLLAR

This perfume-emmitting, anti-barking collar was designed by a biologist in France who studied the reactions of dogs to odours, both positive and negative. He discovered that brief exposure to citronella produces marked avoidance.

At each bark the olfactory collar emits a spray of oil of citronella. The dog quickly establishes the link between the spray of perfume and his barking and chooses to not bark. The collar is activated by a sensitive microphone, which in turn releases a spray of oil stored as an aerosol in its reservoir. We would point out, however, that such collars are at present marketed to suit the pockets of the average dog owner, the workings therefore are not perhaps as highly sophisticated as some of its electronic counterparts and barking by other dogs can activate these units. It may therefore be rendered unsuitable in environments such as boarding kennels. However the sensitivity of this collar's microphone has produced purely by chance a secondary use; whilst being tried on a Border Collie cross, Scamp, for a serious barking problem, the owner pointed out that the dog also liked destroying items posted through the letter box. The collar produced a good result with the barking problem so it was decided to try this device with the "post" situation as the dog previously barked before devouring the mail. On this occasion, however, the dog did not bark having previously been conditioned by the collar, but hurdled head long into the door at which point the collar was activated by the impact, putting Scamp off his favourite pastime! Initial tests by the writers of this book have found this very new product to be effective on most dogs whilst affording less controversy than its electric counterpart.

WAYS TO COPE WITH THE ESCAPE ARTIST

The first and logical step with an escape artist is to secure your perimeter with high fencing. However, this is often not practical and can be expensive and aesthetically displeasing.

The Cattle Fence (Low Voltage Only)

This has been employed for many years with reasonable success to contain dogs within a permitted perimeter. The wire, normally orange coloured, can become an indicator to the dog and tests suggest that even when this fence is switched off, the dog has enormous respect and does not go near the wire. However, such devices do not deter the "high jumper" or "burrower"!

The Invisible Fence

This is a very up-market version of the cattle fence in which a cable is run around the perimeter and can be buried beneath the soil. The dog wears a small electronic collar that emits an auditory signal should the dog approach the perimeter, which would then be followed up with a shock should the dog decide to proceed

ULTRA-SONIC DOG WHISTLE. This whistle works at a frequency of around the 15kHz cycle. Illustration by G. Horn.

further. These types are exceptionally effective but are a costly alternative.

WHISTLES

There are three main types of dog whistles, the ultra-sonic (often called the Silent Dog Whistle), the Shepherd's Penny Whistle and the Gun Dog Whistle.

The Ultra-Sonic Whistle

For general training purposes, this whistle can prove a very valuable training aid, although in the initial stages of training, the voice command is still most important as, unlike the whistle, emotional tonal values can be used to induce response.

Whilst the ultra-sonic whistle lacks the tonal value of the voice, it does offer some inherent advantages. A popular misconception about these whistles is that owners feel all dogs in the locality will come running to them or that the whistle is a magic remedy to call the dog back to you. It is not. It is merely a training aid and a substitute for the human voice. Neither is this whistle silent, of course, but works at a frequency of around the 15 kHz cycle.

This is well within the hearing capabilities of dogs who are purported to be able to hear a frequency as high as 100 kHz, although most experts believe 30 kHz to be a more likely level. The 15 kHz frequency, therefore, is unlikely to be audible to an older person although many children are able to hear this sound. Do not be confused by the air venting from the whistle as being the sound emitted by this device or worry that the whistle is working correctly since a blow of the whistle should produce a visible reaction from your dog. The pitch can be adjusted to obtain the maximum reaction.

Fifteen kHz is a useful frequency for such a device. This is, in effect, a short-wave signal, which will carry a great distance compared with the human voice. This becomes even more evident where the sound is diminished by weather conditions, such as fog or snow, or where sounds may be deflected, such as in wooded areas.

This device becomes extremely useful when used as a homing signal for the dog and can prove far less embarrassing than repeatedly calling your dog with your voice. Areas, such as public parks where a high ambient sound level may be expected, give us another opportunity to use an ultra-sonic whistle as the frequency will be far less confused with other sounds.

Remember, this is not a magical device. It may attract your dog's attention in the short term, but in order to explore its full potential, the dog, as with all other training, must be taught to respond correctly.

For the older dog, ultra-sonic whistles can prove advantageous, as, unlike humans, whose high frequency hearing diminishes with age, a dog's hearing diminishes at the lower frequencies. Thus many old dogs may be able to hear such whistles where lower frequencies may be inaudible to them.

The Shepherd's Penny Whistle

This is sometimes called the mouth whistle. On asking a shepherd recently why the whistle was worn on a cord around his neck, a serious reply was given to the effect that it was to stop him from swallowing this device. So specialised is the nature of its use and difficulty of operation that we are omitting further explanation. Should you have keen interest in this use, do find a shepherd to teach you.

The Gun Dog Whistle

This whistle and other whistles that can be heard by dog and human alike have advantages over the human voice in similar situations to those where the ultra-sonic whistle can be used, for example, on a shoot where sounds of guns firing, beaters, shouts, etc., may be heard. This signal will be more clearly distinguishable to the dog than that of the human voice.

This type of whistle and the combination whistle, which emits both high and low pitch sounds, can be used in a multitude of ways for such things as recall, re-direction, etc.

THE SHEPHERD'S PENNY WHISTLE, otherwise known as the mouth whistle.

THE GUN DOG WHISTLE is obtainable as ultra high pitch, high pitch and standard type. Illustrations by G. Horn.

Canine Commands

About half of all owners believe that their dogs understand every word spoken. The other half are of the contrary belief that their dogs do not understand any words. It is most important when starting training your dog to comprehend that the latter is in fact nearer the truth. We therefore mainly use language to communicate with the dog out of pure convenience to ourselves. It is more socially acceptable, for example outside a shop, to tell our dog to "sit" and "stay" rather than use a command such as "sky blue pink", which would work equally as well but would cause many a raised eyebrow from passers by. We therefore adopt the easiest option which is to use our native tongue. A dog, therefore, hearing only a *sound* will be stimulated by correct training to respond accordingly. However we must always remember to use clearly defined sounds and, of course, consistent ones.

Barbara Woodhouse made famous the expression, "Sit with a T, dear", a most sensible use of the word as other commands commonly used, such as "stand" and "stay" may be easily confused in the dog's mind. A classic example of confusion arose when a Dobermann developed a serious recall problem. The dog's family consisted of six people, all of whom took turns to take the dog for its recreation. On investigating the problem with each individual member of the family, it was found that they all used different commands, tones of voice and body signals to get their dog to return. On teaching the owners to use one command, one tone of voice and consistent body gestures, the problem was soon resolved. *Tell* your dog, don't ask him.

Whilst dogs may be limited in their understanding of words, they certainly have an uncanny awareness of emotions. Your dog will certainly pick up authority in your voice as it will also understand your pleasure or displeasure in given situations. The use of voice becomes particularly important on recall where total interaction will encourage the dog towards you.

However, verbal commands are only one means of stimulation and indeed people with a speech disability should still have success with training using hand commands and body language. Whistles are often used, particularly for recall training and in specialist fields such as sheep and gun dog work. Hand signals are often employed by obedience competitors in order that the dog may not be confused at competition venues, such as Crufts, where high noise levels are encountered. Military and police dogs are also trained in this way in view of the many situations where voice commands would be totally inappropriate. Even with such hand signals, a positive body action will be more effective than

SEMPER PARATUS. Dogs are loyal and obedient companions whose greatest joy is pleasing their owners. Photo by P. Aze.

an insipid gesture. This is even more relevant when using your voice, so be positive. Tell your dog, don't ask it, but be kind. Continual and unnecessary yelling at your dog will result in one that is so habituated towards this stimulation that when a necessary situation develops, such as stopping it from running into a road, his reaction will be dulled to a point of refusal.

Suggested List of Commands

LEAVE—Possibly the most useful of all commands; use to stop sniffing, pulling or running towards another dog or when catching your dog devouring the Sunday roast.

HEEL—Positional command on stepping off, also to keep your dog by your side. (Dog's front paws should be level with owner.)

SIT—Sit. (Accentuate the sound "it".)

FLAT/DOWN/LIE—Used to put dog in flat position. "down" may be used. However, if your dog has a jumping up problem necessitating the use of the word "down", then another command should be used for the lying down position.

STAND—Stand. (Accentuate the sound "and".)

WAIT—Temporary command used in "sit", "flat" or "stand" position, when you will be asking your dog to move off again shortly.

STAY—Used to leave your dog in "sit", "flat" or "stand" position, usually for longer periods of time when you will be returning to your dog. (Accentuate the sound "ay".)

COME—Used for recall, preceded by dog's name, i.e., "Bonzo, come".

HEEL QUICKLY—On moving off only, when running/jogging with your dog.

HEEL SLOWLY—On moving off only, when walking slowly. Useful on ice, slippery embankments, etc.

QUIET—Command to stop unwanted barking.

SPEAK—Command to encourage barking.

FETCH, HOLD, GIVE—Used in retrieving. Give may also be used when taking any item from your dog.

GO SEEK—Used in tracking and searching.

WATCH—Used in guard work.

AWAY—Used for send-away.

UP/THROUGH/OVER—Used for agility.

READY TO GO. Remember to praise your dog lavishly whenever he obeys your command. Photo by M. Mohamed.

Training a Dog Is Like Cutting a Diamond

A diamond cutter is a skilled craftsman who can create a beautiful gem, but in the wrong hands the stone can become worthless dust.

Before you train your dog either on your own, at a club or with professional help, consider your dog's individual personality, his physical abilities and mental agility and be sympathetically understanding of any defects that may impair his progress.

A good trainer will tailor the training to suit the individual dog, just as a diamond cutter will study the stone carefully before cutting.

A LITTLE GEM. This talented terrier is clearing the bar jump. Photo by M. Fellows.

A WHEEL TREAT. This Airedale is coming through the tire jump. Photo by K. Taylor.

Body Language, Body Signals and Meaningful Gestures

When running in the park even the domesticated dog (*Canis familiaris*) needs to know, almost instantly, if the approaching dog is friend or foe. He will do this by observing the other dog's body signals, for example an erect tail will indicate the dominant dog whilst the tail between the legs will indicate a subservient creature.

A wagging tail may suggest, "I think you and I will get on, buddy". This gives the trainer and behaviourist a good insight into the dog's character and his intended next move. The "clued-up" owner will be wise to study such signals to tell, for example, if their dog or the other dog is likely

PLAYFUL POSE. Illustration by G. Horn.

to start a confrontation. An understanding of your dog's body language will lead you to better understanding, greater security, and an ability to ensure the unexpected becomes expected!

BODY SIGNALS: THE POSITIVE EFFECT

This uncanny ability our dogs have to perceive body signals can help us greatly in training. For example, if I consistently step off on my left leg when requiring my dog to walk to heel, this will soon become a signal for my dog to move off. This will in time reduce the necessity for one of the "heel" commands to be used, important for both the obedience competitor (not allowed to use additional auditory commands) and very useful to the average owner who wishes to minimise the use of such commands.

Dogs inherently follow the left leg when stepping off (if they are worked on the left). How often will owners step off on the right leg to find the dog is 2 feet (60 centimetres) behind them and proceed to check them forwards when in fact the owner was at fault or misunderstood by the dog?

NOTE: The check chain should never be used when stepping off to stimulate the dog into action. After all, he has done nothing wrong, he has simply misunderstood your

SUBMISSIVE POSE.

DOMINANT POSE.

AGGRESSIVE POSE.
Illustrations by G. Horn.

body signals or lacks motivation.

HAND SIGNALS

Rule one: if the dog is not watching you then the hand signal will not work!

The Sit

The palm should be upright. Starting at waist level, raise the arm briskly to shoulder level, accompanied to begin with the addition of the auditory command "sit".

With your dog watching your hand (food or a favourite toy may be used as an inducement to begin with, thereby encouraging him to watch your hand), raise your hand and the dog's head will automatically go up and its bottom go down, thus into the "sit" position.

It is unlikely that any physical putting into the "sit" will be necessary, but if it is do so. Clearly the dog who does not respond to food motivation, i.e., has a low appetite threshold, will not benefit from the use of food in these exercises.

THE SIT HAND SIGNAL. Illustration by G. Horn.

FROM SIT OR STAND TO FLAT HAND SIGNAL. Illustration by G. Horn.

The Flat

The palm is now facing down. Starting at shoulder height, lower the arm briskly to between waist and knee level. Accompanied in the beginning by the auditory command "flat," "down" or "lie" (which ever you have chosen to use).

The dog must again be watching your hand and, as before, food may be used. Lowering your hand will automatically cause the dog to assume the flat position. However, some pressure on the back with your hand may assist in this exercise.

The Stand

Although hand signals may be commonly used by obedience competitors it is not an aid to the dog to respond, merely a convenient compromise between sit and flat signals.

The Come

Imagine you are seeing your loved one after some years, they are rushing through the airport lounge, you will probably open your arms as a welcoming gesture. This applies equally when calling your dog towards you. The outstretched arms coming towards your middle has therefore become the normal body signal to call your dog in order to produce a welcoming effect.

On your dog's arrival both hands are raised up towards the chin thereby encouraging the "sit" presentation.

Stay/Wait

Spread your fingers and thrust the palm of your hand towards the dog's nose. This will cause him to blink or throw his head slightly backwards ensuring a greater level of attention.

NOTE: Use of the hand to reinforce the "stay" or "wait" commands will have a highly desirable secondary effect. The dog will perceive such hand movements in a positive fashion and not as a threat from the instigator. Children and those inexperienced with dogs often make such violent movements towards an unsuspecting or suspicious dog. The use of the hand in this way will desensitise your dog towards such movement. The dog will perceive oncoming hands in association with positive command controls rather than in the negative response of hostility.

Steadying

Following on the "stay/wait" command, the hand may be raised with fingers spread to steady the dog when walking away.

HAND SIGNAL FOR THE RECALL (COME). Illustration by G. Horn.

THE STAY/WAIT HAND SIGNAL.

THE STAND. Illustrations by G. Horn

The Biddable Dog

"WILL TRAINING AFFECT MY DOG'S CHARACTER?"

Yes, but only for the better. Kind training bonds owner and dog, it encourages security in the dog's mind and it will enable the dog to have a much fuller life, joining you in events that an untrained dog would not be able to attend. Dogs do enjoy the special time you give them in training sessions. It most certainly will not make the happy dog less happy or the affectionate dog less loving. Many dogs, like many children, are born into this world biddable and cooperative. But it is wrong to assume that a less biddable dog or a less cooperative child is so because of its owner or parent. Many owners, like many parents, do all the right things but alas X, the unknown factor, has its role to play.

This chapter, however, is dedicated to the owner with the well-balanced dog. Whilst equally applicable to the problem-dog owner, they may need to go further with the training or seek professional advice from a veterinary surgeon, behaviourist or professional trainer.

Learning to drive a car/automobile by reading a book would be considered most impractical, thus few books have ventured into this type of training. Teaching a dog is comparable and many people are frustrated by the simplicity of some dog training books and their own resulting lack of success. Our aim in this publication is to go further into the complexities of this subject, but it is still of paramount importance that groundwork training is carried out and only after considerable efforts should the owner contemplate more complex training methods. Consistency is the key to good training.

HEEL WORK

Most owners will only see the necessity to teach a dog to walk to heel as a means of stopping the dog from pulling. It is, however, the most convenient method of establishing subordination. Many owners of small dogs therefore forego this aspect of training viewing it as unnecessary and ironically many of the smaller breeds display greater dominance problems than larger breeds. Similarly people whose lives do not necessitate lead-walking (those utilising cars to the recreation area and those with extensive gardens or land) may also suffer such problems.

Basic Heel Work Training

The well-dressed dog handler wears neat, close-fitting clothes so that his attire does not flap in the dog's face causing unnecessary distraction.

There is nothing wrong in practising heel work in your garden but without greater stimulation and distractions a true response will probably not be evident and many dogs resent this type of training in their own homes manifesting itself in a lethargic response, often to the point of laying down and refusing to move. Whilst this behaviour should not be tolerated, a more stimulating environment will help. *It is easier to train a pulling dog than a lagging dog.* First you will need to acquire a slip collar, a half-check collar or full check chain. The minimum degree of compulsion is desirable. It is perfectly possible, for example, to train a dog on its ordinary collar. Should the dog then show only a slight tendency to pull, a slip collar or half-check would be preferable and if pulling persists a full check chain would be necessary. *WARNING:* Check chains should only be used on dogs from a minimum of six months of age.

It is normal to walk a dog on the left-hand side. Swapping sides, even though pavement walking on narrow country lanes, for example, can become more difficult, is still undesirable and causes confusion to the dog. Owners who walk two dogs simultaneously should first practise heel work individually, the most capable dog eventually being trained to the right side.

Your dog must be taught to walk at your pace in the direction you desire. It is easy, for example, when practising heel work in a park, to assume that you are obtaining a standard far higher than would be perceived by an onlooker.

Try practising your heel work using the lines of a football pitch or tennis court, if available. You may be surprised how far your dog has caused you to drift off course.

With your dog on your left side and the check chain correctly fitted, training may commence. The idea is not to allow the check chain to tighten around your dog's neck. This is why trainers are upset at the definition "choke chain" as it implies such an action taking place. A tight check chain will create worse pulling. Try putting a check chain over a friend's arm and pulling. You will notice as the chain tightens, your friend will pull his arm away from you in exactly the same way as a dog will try to pull away from that choking sensation. Think of a *check* as being similar to a light smack.

BAD BACKS START WITH BAD HANDLING

First it must be firmly established in your mind that the intention of the lead and check chain is *not* to hold back or pull your dog into position. A loose check chain with a check applied at the correct time will do infinitely more good. Jerking the lead backwards will impose unnecessary strain on the handler's back and shoulder. The preferred method of checking is to hold the lead in both hands, applying a check with the left hand across the handler's body. It is also important that the left hand is placed *over* the lead as inverted wrists can easily be damaged if the dog makes a sudden pull. Do not fiddle with the lead and check chain, particularly any rings, and keep all fingers over the lead with only the thumb underneath.

METHOD: Commence by stepping off on your left leg, accompanied with the command "heel".

NOTE: movement of the left leg will eventually become a body signal for your dog to move off. Should your dog go ahead on the lead, with speed and dexterity, you should give him a short sharp check accompanied with the command "heel". If your dog assumes the correct position (your dog's front legs beside your legs), then *praise* him with a tone demonstrating great pleasure. Conversely, a lack of response should be met with a further, slightly firmer check and a repeat of the command "heel" with a strong tone. Although some dogs will respond in a matter of minutes to this stimulation, many more owners will find that weeks will have to be spent on this exercise before results occur. Persevere!

As well as walking your dog at the normal pace, slow and fast paces should also be practised.

Slow Pace

This can prove invaluable when walking on slippery surfaces, such as ice or a muddy embankment and it is of course necessary for the less physically able owner. Almost everyone will experience a situation, such as walking in a crowded street,

where time given to this exercise will be amply rewarded.

The method of correction checking, for example, is identical to normal heel work practice. Still step off on your left leg but the accompanying command should now be "heel slowly".

This exercise, initially, can prove frustrating as dogs become quickly bored at this pace and may start sniffing at the ground or looking around for further stimulation. Limit the training period of this exercise in its early stages to no more than a couple of minutes. Try to keep leg movements flowing as jerky movements will result in your dog being confused.

Fast Pace

You are faced with a situation on a busy main road where crossing speedily is essential. This is not the time to begin practising a fast pace with your dog! This should have been taught before it became necessary and is yet another aspect of essential control. With your dog on your left side, leading with your left foot and giving the command "heel quickly", commence at a jogging pace. This is not the four-minute mile!

Initially most dogs will become very bouncy during this exercise and will tend to leap up at the owners and bite the lead in their excitement. Most handlers tend to over-correct their dogs on this exercise. It is far easier when the dog becomes less controllable to revert to the normal pace, resuming fast pace when the dog has settled. Fast pace will increase the dog's metabolic rate and in turn his hormone production. This exercise, therefore, will tend to exaggerate problems in the hyper-sexual dog.

Using Fast Pace as a Motivator

The excitement this exercise generates can be used to great advantage to motivate the lagging dog. This problem can be particularly manifest in breeds such as Labradors who go from pulling to lagging at the blink of an eye. Owners tend to slow to the dog's pace, which simply exacerbates the problem. Breaking into a trot can motivate a dog in a most desirable fashion.

Out with the Family

When walking your dog during the early days of training it will certainly be helpful if other members of the group stay beside or behind you. This is particularly true of children who are playing ahead of you. The dog in this situation will naturally want to be "in on the action".

It is reasonable however in the later stages of training to expect your dog to walk properly irrespective of other stimulations.

SIT

Under normal circumstances, of course, teaching your dog to sit is a highly desirable exercise. However, certain categories of dog should be exempt, such as dogs who may have inherent hip problems (English Mastiffs, etc.) and dogs required for showing, where excessive use of the "sit"

Begin heel training by stating the command "heel" and stepping off on your left leg. Photo by R. Hutchings.

Your dog should remain directly at your side, not lagging behind or pulling ahead. Photo by R. Hutchings.

Keeping your dog by your side allows you more control over him. Photo by R. Hutchings.

command may cause them to default to this position in the show ring. Another classic problem is with the Dobermann Pinscher who suffers from a syndrome known as "the Dobermann swing". On sitting, their bodies swing round to face the owner, so careful attention should be paid to correcting this fault on a continual basis until the dog is approximately two years of age.

METHOD: From a stationary position, a gentle pulling upward movement of the lead in the right hand combined with pushing and guiding the dog's bottom with the flat of your left hand, accompanied with the auditory command "sit" should produce a good result. When sitting the dog whilst on the move, tell your dog to "sit" two paces before you intend stopping. This will roughly allow for the time the message takes to reach his ears, travel through his brain and transmit to his backside! Failure to do this results in the dog being two steps ahead of the owner and having to step backwards to be beside the owner, which can prove most inconvenient particularly in the case of a kerbside drill.

SIT/STAY

Having achieved the sitting position you can now proceed to teach your dog the "sit/stay".

METHOD: With your dog sitting, use the auditory command "stay" accompanied with a hand signal. Hold the lead in the left and right hand with an "elbow" in the lead. The check chain cross-over point should be at the top of the dog's neck.

The owner should now proceed to move around the dog clockwise and correct the dog with an upward check and a reinforcement of the "stay" command should he move. If your dog is unhappy or disturbed by you going behind, a three-quarter arc is suggested, alternating clockwise and counter-clockwise.

If your dog has already laid down or is almost down, do not pull up on the check chain—it may cause neck damage. Once you are able to move around your dog three times, it is now time, whilst holding the lead, to move out in front of your dog. When teaching your dog to "stay," stand side-on. This produces less body area for your dog to be attracted to and is less likely to induce confusion with the "recall" exercises. Eye contact should also be avoided as this again encourages your dog towards you. React speedily if he moves and put him back on the exact spot from which he moved.

On returning to your dog's right side, try to ensure that he stays in the position in which he was left. Stand beside him, take a pace away to your right then a pace back to him (to your left) then lavishly praise your dog. This method has proved to stabilise the dog on returning. Teaching your dog to stay requires time and patience.

Leaving a dog in a "stay"

position for excessive times and distances too early on during training may produce a very unstable and worried dog. Gradually increase the time from 30 seconds to eventually five minutes for this exercise, by ten seconds every third day.

Likewise, distance may be increased by one pace each week, but if your dog is looking distressed ease up on this exercise.

It may prove helpful to have a chart registering time and distance achieved each day for both "sit/stay" and "flat" exercises. *NOTE: Overheated dogs will tend to drop easily into the "down" position. We would advise limiting this exercise in very warm weather.* An eventual competitive standard of a ten-minute out-of-sight "sit/stay" will be the aim of the more ambitious handler.

THE LYING POSITION

A very necessary exercise to teach your dog apart from its usefulness particularly when combined with the "stay" command, this position certainly is the most subservient position for the dog to be in and is therefore useful as a "dominance" exercise.

A lady with a Great Dane of a somewhat dominant disposition, on a suggestion from the

SIT/STAY. The time and distance used when practicing the "sit/stay" can be increased gradually. A chart measuring both time and distance may prove helpful. Photo by J. Combe.

instructor not to continue the exercise (after ten minutes' effort to no avail), spent 30 minutes determined to win over her dog. She achieved a two-minute stay and from that day on her dog became far more biddable in all aspects (Full marks for perseverance).

There are numerous methods to achieve the lying position but the two most popular are as follows.

METHOD 1: With your dog on your left and sitting, hold the lead in your right hand, the lowest point of the lead and chain should be approximately three-quarters of the dog's shoulder height above ground. Your left foot now applies downward pressure until your dog lays down. Additional pressure on the dog's back with the left hand may also be required. Don't forget to praise your dog as soon as he responds but do not over-excite him as this may cause him to jump straight back up again. This method, however, is not suitable for some larger breeds, particularly if the owner is of a delicate physique. Its advantage, however, is fast response and does not require the owner to continually bend down.

METHOD 2: Again with the dog in a sitting position at your left side, note whether your dog is leaning inwards or away from you. Place the left hand on the dog's back and lift the nearer front paw (if leaning in) or the further front paw (if leaning out) and roll the dog towards you or

away from you respectively.

Please note that the paw should be lifted up 2 to 3 inches from the ground so the knee is bent. As your face may be level with the dog during this exercise, under no circumstances should this method be adopted on a snappy or aggressive dog.

Never pull both front legs away from the dog simultaneously. This could result in injury to the dog.

FLAT/STAY

Rules applied in the "sit/stay" still apply, fast response to breaking stay by voice and action (if necessary), replacement to original position, stand side-on to dog and no eye contact. The walking-around exercise offers little benefit as a check cannot readily be applied for correction. Auditory commands may be "down", "flat" or "lie". "Down" is not suitable if the dog is prone to jumping up as most people will automatically revert to this as a correctional command to "get down" only serving to confuse the dog.

The expected duration in this position can be doubled from that of the "sit/stay" exercise.

As the dog becomes stable in this position it is advantageous to practice in busy areas such as parks and enlist the help of friends to step over your dog. This proves most useful particularly if your dog is to be tied outside busy venues such as shops. The ambitious owner may in time aim for a 20-minute out-of-sight "stay".

TOTAL CONTROL CONCEPT. Practice the "flat/stay" with distractions. This will prove helpful when you bring your dog to public places. Photo by J. Combe.

COME—RECALLING YOUR DOG

Puppies

We can often be misguided by the behaviour of the young puppy who will often cling to his owner showing no inclination to leave his side. It can come as a shock to the owner who has hitherto said "my puppy always comes back" when his dog suddenly decides that other dogs and stimuli are as much or more fun than he is! We would therefore urge that even the clingy puppy be trained to recall.

From as little as three months

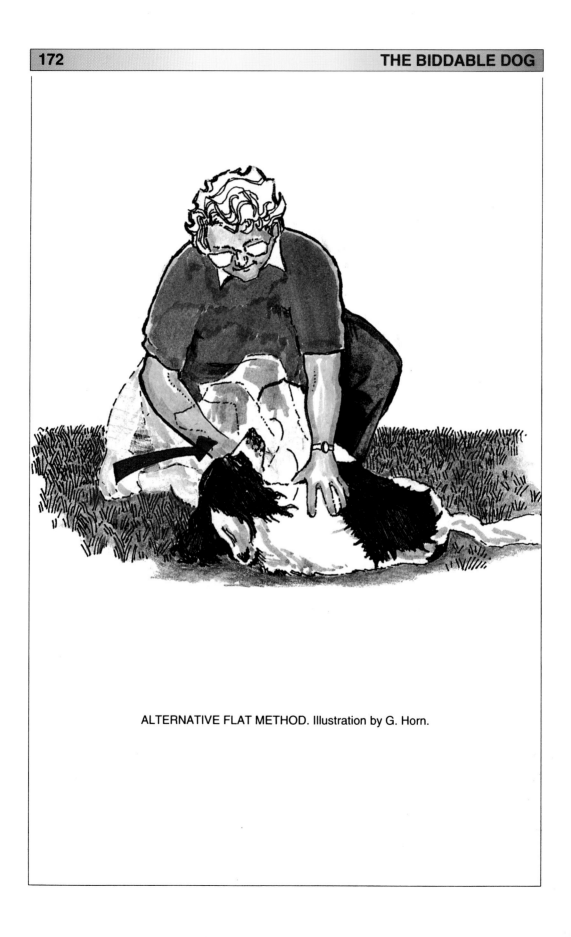

ALTERNATIVE FLAT METHOD. Illustration by G. Horn.

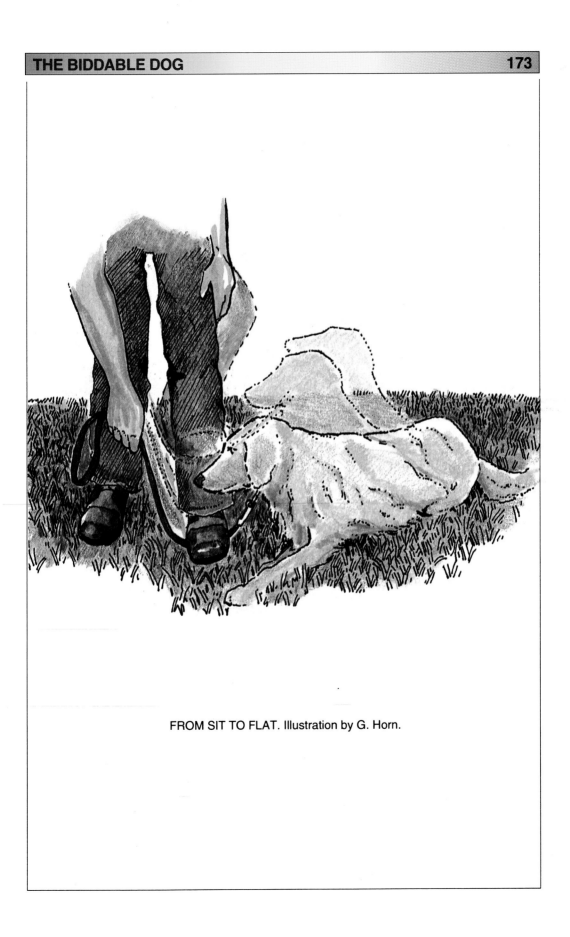

FROM SIT TO FLAT. Illustration by G. Horn.

ON YOUR MARK. The first step in recall training on the lead is to make your dog sit and wait. Photo by R. Hutchings.

LEAD TRAINING

Tell your dog to "sit" and "wait" (the wait command is in effect a short-term stay and is followed by subsequent commands). Go to the end of the lead, turn and face your dog and after a brief delay call him to you as before, "Bonzo, come". At this stage encouragement is the order of the day. After a couple of weeks, however, you may like to have the dog sitting in front of you. Rather than nagging the dog with yet another command, try rubbing its back as you praise him, simultaneously positioning him in the "sit", but this time without auditory command. The presentation will soon become quite habitual.

LINE TRAINING

Although similar to the lead training, a 20-foot line is attached to an immovable object, such as a fence post, tree, etc. The line is attached to an ordinary collar (*NOT A CHECK CHAIN*). The dog may be told to "sit" and "wait", as in the lead training, or it may be allowed to wander, both types of training being equally beneficial. This exercise is now a hands-free operation as calling the dog will require proper use of your voice and good interaction, but with the comfort of knowing that your dog is unable to bolt off. Should the dog not initially respond it may be necessary to pick up the line and pull or guide him towards you, but if the puppy and lead training

of age a puppy should be given infant recall training exercises. The puppy "recall", so called, involves the following.

METHOD: With your dog on a normal collar and leash, walk along a few paces (the quality of heel work does not matter for this exercise). Then suddenly run backwards (yes—we do mean backwards) calling your puppy to you using first his name then the auditory command, "Bonzo, come". Gather the lead and make a huge fuss on your puppy's arrival in front of you. This should be a fun exercise. Do not discourage a nice bouncy "recall", neither bother with such things as the dog sitting in front of you at this stage of its training. At five to six months of age this training may be formalised.

have been successful, this should be unnecessary. *PLEASE* be careful, particularly with the strong, fast dog, that you do not find yourself in a position where the line can trip you, strangers or other dogs.

Make sure your dog stays within range of the line and does not check itself inadvertently. If you feel your dog is now ready to be let off the leash, make sure firstly that one hundred per cent success in your garden is evident. If your dog does not respond in this environment, your chances of success in a more stimulating environment are negligible. Clearly the time must come when your dog is let off its leash in a recreational area. At this point your heart will probably miss a beat but, providing you have done all the basic ground work and remember the following points, "recall" should be straightforward. Your dog is now free and there is not likely to be any form of compulsion available to you. It is equally unlikely that you will catch a dog that does not wish to return to you and who is chasing around a field at 20 miles an hour! The only tool now

GOOD BOY! Praise is the most important part of training. Every time your dog comes to you reward and encourage him. Photo by K. Taylor.

available for "recall" training will be the use of your voice and total interaction with your dog is necessary. Call your dog, "Bonzo, come". If Bonzo responds and is coming towards you, encourage him with copious praise. If Bonzo is ignoring you, reinforce the command with a much stronger tone and repeat the command. As he then turns and comes in your direction, encourage again. Try to stand your ground, running after a dog will be considered as a great game by him. Running away from him should encourage him towards you but assumes of course that your dog is looking at or for you, as does lying on the ground or hiding. *However long it may take to "recall" your dog, never scold him upon his return. Remember, a dog has very short association time and punishment may be associated with the action of returning.*

Don't forget, after training, play with your dog or let him play with other dogs.

A point to remember. After your first successful "recall" you are likely to want to put your dog back on the lead as you now feel secure in the fact that there is no longer a risk to his return. *Try to avoid this.* Instead take courage and let him go again and repeat this exercise for half a dozen times before restricting him to the lead. Your dog will be less likely therefore to associate the recall with the unpleasant experience of walkies over. This formula should be adopted throughout the young dog's life.

YOU CALLED? The last step of recall training on the lead is to use the "come" command and your dog should follow suit. Don't forget to praise him! Photo by R. Hutchings.

Facing page: STEADY AS YOU GO...The second step in recall training on the lead is to go to the end of the lead and face your dog.

More Advanced Training

HEEL WORK

Simply practising heel work by walking in straight lines and circles will not only become boring for ourselves but equally so for our dogs. The intelligent dog will require more than walking around a village hall for an hour.

Right Turns

How often do you see an owner turning a sharp corner only to find the dog three feet from their side and people around muttering "You should keep that dog under control". Particularly for responsible urban dog ownership it is important to practise manoeuvres that may occur in everyday life. With your dog walking beside you at the normal pace, give the auditory command "heel" two paces before you intend turning. Remember it takes time for your command to get from your dog's ears, through its brain to whichever part of its anatomy has to move. Do not check the dog before executing the turn. Always give the dog the benefit of the doubt. However, having turned some 20 to 30 degrees, if your dog is not with you, then check him. After the turn, praise him. Remember to keep the turns neat and tidy, a smart dog only being a reflection of a smart owner.

On this type of turn and about turns, the dog will have further to travel than you. Slow down so that the dog can keep a constant speed, otherwise after execution of the turn the dog will be in an accelerated mode and will promptly go ahead necessitating an unwarranted correction.

About Turns (to the right)

It is very likely that you will find yourself at some time in a restricted area such as a narrow pavement where precision will render benefit to you, your dog and passers-by. The rules of this exercise are the same as for the right turn but do remember to turn tightly 180 degrees. It is all too easy to believe that you have executed the perfect turn only to have it pointed out by an observer that you have taken a 6-foot turning circle. Try practising on the lines of a football pitch or tennis court if available.

Double About Turns

Whilst useful as a training aid they are much more difficult to execute than an ordinary about turn (accentuating any faults) and we do not suggest any practical use for this exercise.

This exercise requires a 360-degree turn, the owner having completed the turn should now be walking in the same direction as when the exercise commenced.

TURN-STYLE. Left turns with your dog can be tricky. Make sure you bring your left leg in front of your dog's chest before actually turning your body. Photo by I. Francais.

Left Turns

This is perhaps one of the most dangerous manoeuvres, particularly with a small dog, so often ending up with the owner tripping. For this exercise a body signal is induced in the form of the left leg coming round in front of the dog's chest before your body actually turns. So whilst walking the dog give the auditory command "heel" as the left foot is forward, take another step on the right foot and bring your left leg around in front of the dog.

This exercise does of course assume that before commencement the dog is correctly to the "heel" position and not pulling.

Bending the left knee and keeping your foot near the ground will reduce the risk of accidentally tripping.

Owners of two dogs should particularly practise this exercise especially where dogs are walked on either side.

Turning right with a dog on your right hand side should be executed in the same way as the left turn.

Left About Turn

The object of this exercise is to turn 180 degrees, but this time into the dog. A left wheel is the normal order of the day, often occupying a space of 6 feet to turn in. *This is not a true left about turn.*

The auditory command for this

exercise is "back" as in order to maintain the "heel" position the dog will have to physically move backwards out of your way. Unlike all other exercises a gentle pull back on the lead and check chain is required.

This exercise will have enormous benefits for the owners of pulling dogs, will teach the dominant dogs subservience and is essential for the owner who takes more than one dog out for a walk at a time.

Should your dog suffer from conditions in its back legs and hips, such as arthritis and hip dysplasia, then no more than a couple of turns of this type per day should be practised or an alternative left about turn may be adopted.

German Left About Turn

This turn is ideal for dogs such as German Shepherds as it does not impose as much strain upon the back legs as the conventional left about turn. Whilst turning into your dog he is brought around behind you so when your 180 degree turn is complete, your dog is again on your left side ("heel" position). This exercise, when practised on the lead, is similar to that of the finish described later.

Heel Free (heel work OFF the lead)

By the time you consider

LIFE IS FULL OF TURNS. Practicing turns can prove quite helpful if you are planning to show your dog. Photo by I. Francais.

practising this exercise your dog should be walking nicely on a loose lead. To begin with, leave the lead and check chain on your dog and put the other end of the lead in your pocket, or tucked into a belt. It now of course becomes more important that body signals and erratic use of the arms be controlled, your major tool now being your *voice*. Should this training be successful with little or no use of the lead having been necessary, you may now commence heel free exercises with the lead removed.

With your dog sitting calmly beside you, hold the slip collar/ half check/check chain to begin, step off on your left leg accompanied with the auditory command "heel" and proceed to walk in a defined but easy pattern, such as a circle. You will probably find a clockwise direction easier for this exercise. Should your dog be responding well, you may let go of the collar/chain, put your left hand on your left thigh and use your voice to encourage your dog's performance. The initial holding of the chain of course will soon become unnecessary.

At this stage should lead training have been carried out properly then it is unlikely that this transition will pose any problem at all. However, those who have misused check chains by checking the dog when stepping off and before execution of turns will experience far more difficulty.

TIDYING UP THE RECALL

When we began training the prime objective was getting your dog back and giving him plenty of praise in order to encourage him. But now you may wish to formalise the "recall" perhaps with the intention of competition work. We must therefore go back to lead training, now ensuring the dog finishes "recall" by sitting neatly in front of us. Should your dog consistently sit skew-whiff then the following should correct this problem. If the dog is sitting with its backside to your left, then your right leg should be brought back as he comes towards your front and conversely if the dog is sitting with its head to your left side, then your left leg should be brought back. Repetitive correction will encourage neat presentation but should never be perceived by the dog as constant nagging or recalling will suffer.

THE FINISH

With your dog sitting in front of you after "recall" you will probably require him to walk around the back of you to the "heel" position. This type of finish is more commonly used worldwide than the German finish, where the dog swings around in front of you and, although the result is the same, we feel the conventional finish to be neater and of more use in everyday life. Do try to avoid dragging your dog around or checking him. This does not result in a dog doing happy finishes.

With the dog sitting in front of you, hold the lead in your right hand. Pass the lead behind your back and put the end into your left hand whilst holding the lead part of the way down in your right hand.

Step back on your right leg in conjunction with the auditory command "heel" and walk back as far, and only as far, as is necessary to get your dog to your right side. At this point immediately walk forward, swapping the lead to the left hand, and again going only as far as is necessary to bring your dog to your left side. Your dog should be encouraged to sit beside you, which may involve swapping the lead to the right hand in order that his bottom may be guided down with your left hand.

The object of this exercise is to encourage your dog around to "heel" in the nicest possible way. Soon your dog will be able to carry out this exercise without the necessity of you moving or with the aid of the lead.

STAY

It should now be your intention, should you wish to compete in obedience or working trials that your dog is stable under all conditions. This should include "staying" in the presence of other dogs, even when the other dogs are mobile, "staying" whilst being distracted by people stepping over or walking around him and even "staying" when a gun has been fired.

Many an obedience competitor has found that because the dog has caught sight of a member of the family outside the competition area, "stays" have been broken as the dog has gone to greet them. Practise with distractions such as other members of the family suddenly appearing in order that this embarrassing situation does not happen to you.

At a presentation for the Police Dog of the Year Award at the Metropolitan Police Training Establishment, Hendon, England, whilst being awarded the top prize, the dog bolted off to see the policeman's wife whom he spotted in the audience, causing much embarrassment.

RETRIEVE

Perhaps you will want your dog to retrieve simply for fun or you may wish to compete in working trials, obedience trials or field trials. Whichever the case, retrieving can be great fun for both you and your dog. It should be understood at this point that certain breeds will of course respond much better to this training than others, the retriever breeds for example being superb at such exercises whilst the German Shepherd and Border Collie may require more practice and patient handling. It is always advantageous to use a purpose-made dumbbell as it gives the dog the best possible item to hold comfortably and without dropping, the height of the stem making it easy for the dog to pick it up off the ground. It is also exceedingly practical when making the dog "give" the object, if he is not releasing it, a tap on both ends with the palms of your hands simultaneously will release

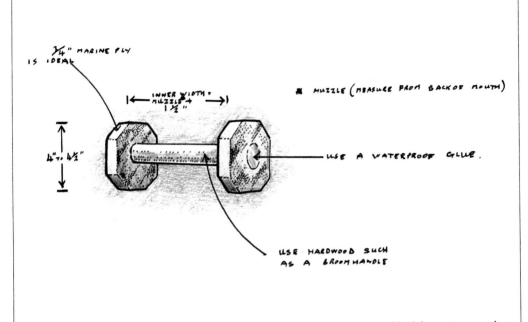

3/4" MARINE PLY IS IDEAL

INNER WIDTH =
MUZZLE +
1 1/2"

4" TO 4 1/2"

M MUZZLE (MEASURE FROM BACK OF MOUTH)

USE A WATERPROOF GLUE.

USE HARDWOOD SUCH AS A BROOM HANDLE

BESPOKE (TAILORMADE) DUMBBELL. This sort of dumbbell is the ideal item to use when practicing retrieving with your dog. Illustration by G. Horn.

your dog's hold on the object. Often gun dog handlers and trainers start off using dummy throw bags but again we suggest that the dumbbell offers most advantages for the novice retriever.

There are many dogs particularly of the gun dog variety such as Labradors and other retrievers and the spaniels who appear enthusiastic and are "natural retrievers". However, a little practice on the lead (on a normal collar, not a check chain) to begin with is always advantageous if we wish to get the best out of our dogs. Commence with your dog by your side (There is no need at this stage for the dog to be formally sitting beside you. This can be polished up when the exercise is firmly established in

the dog's mind). Next, interest your dog with the dumbbell, waving it in front of him and generally teasing a little. Ideally your dog should exhibit interest and excitement at this stage. If not, it is likely that firmer methods may be required. Throw the dumbbell approximately 10 to 15 feet and if your dog runs to it, go with him without restraining him as encouragement is always the key to this exercise wherever possible. The "natural retriever" will almost inevitably pick up the dumbbell. At this stage praise him with your voice only and start running back as with the puppy "recall", gathering the lead as he comes towards you. Again when he is in front of you, do not worry about the "sit" until a much later stage in the training, simply take the dumbbell and make oodles of fuss.

It may, however, be necessary to teach the dog to "hold" and "give" as separate exercises, particularly if your dog is not of a gun dog variety. Have your dog sitting beside you and offer the dumbbell towards his mouth. Ideally the dog should go forward to grab the object, but if no

an item such as an empty cartridge case or in later stages of obedience competitions where the judge will decide on a particular object to be retrieved. Try to always encourage the dog to go forward towards the object, gradually lowering it to ground level as training progresses. It is quite likely that the dog who has had to be so encouraged, when

"FETCH" is the proper command to use when sending your dog to retrieve the dumbbell. Photo by R. Hutchings.

interest is shown open your dog's mouth, roll the dumbbell in and stroke him under the chin both to encourage him and to keep his head up, thus making it impossible for him to drop the item. This exercise is also often necessary as dogs progress to retrieving more difficult objects, such as in working trials where they may be required to pick up

performing the full exercise on lead, may have to be forced to pick the object up by gentle pushing down of the head and placing the object in the dog's mouth.

The dog will require the following auditory commands:

"Fetch", when sending your dog out to the retrieve article.

"Hold", to both induce the pick

"GIVE" is the command to use when you want the dog to give the dumbbell back to you. Photo by R. Hutchings.

up and to retain the dog's grip on the article.

"Give", when requiring the dog to release the article to you.

NOTE: The "hold" command may be accompanied with the "come" command in the early stages of retrieval.

WARNING: Throwing sticks, particularly when the ground is soft, may cause them to lodge vertically and your dog may be seriously injured when excitedly grabbing for the stick under these circumstances.

Because you see a Border Collie performing perfect "heel" work, a Golden Retriever retrieving superbly or a German Shepherd performing superb man-work, remember much of this ability has been genetically inherited. Your dog may not have inherited such abilities but the ability to give you loyalty, love and companionship will surely have been inherited and this is the most important thing.

The Not-So Biddable Dog

If you have a dog that does not fit the biddable dog training section do not despair! Many training books give advice similar to that in our previous section, but what if this does not work?

HEEL WORK—"HE PULLS LIKE A TRAIN" SYNDROME!

For the really difficult puller it is a good idea to invest in a double lead. Such an item will have a clip on either end and is normally 4 to 6 feet in length. One end can be attached to the check chain above the collar position whilst the other end can be attached to the normal collar. A degree of holding the dog back on the collar combined with correct use of the check chain should help to alleviate your problems. This method would also help owners of dogs who pull back on the check chain, which runs the risk of the dog breaking free. Try using minimal collar restraint as the check chain is still the most important tool when teaching your dog proper heel work.

The Magic Turn Method

With this method allow the dog to travel to the end of the lead. At this point the owner turns crisply and walks in the opposite direction whilst checking and reinforcing the "heel" command. This works particularly well on dogs that "blank out" on the lead as it causes considerable confusion in the dog's mind as to why they suddenly find you walking in the opposite direction. This exercise should encourage concentration by your dog.

"But My Dog Still Pulls"

Before you try any more drastic methods of training it may well be worth considering the use of a head restraining collar. In general terms we do not recommend this piece of equipment over conventional equipment in view of its actual lack of value to training. These devices have been known to cause injury if not correctly fitted and they are frequently mistaken for muzzles. This apart, they do have a role to play for the severely pulling dog and whilst the results may not produce a high percentage success rate, it may well prove the answer if your dog continues to pull.

The Refusal

Surely nothing can be more embarrassing than a dog in the High Street, at the dog training club or when practising in the park, lying down and simply refusing to move. Some breeds are particularly prone to this behaviour such as Mastiffs and Labrador Retrievers. Unless your dog is genuinely fatigued or is unwell, it is likely that he is testing your perseverance and tolerance levels. Coaxing him will not help in this situation although motivation, such as a member of the family walking in front of you, may help. But in all situations a check accompanied with a firm command such as "get up" will prove the best course of action to take. A Labrador with such a problem was ordered by the trainer to "upsy daisy". Whilst meant in the best spirit, this particularly lazy dog would later only respond in this situation to this command causing some embarrassment to its owner, especially outside shops.

THE HORMONE FACTOR

Many male dogs of a hyper-sexual nature will show an extreme tendency to pulling. This may often be accompanied by excessive sniffing and urination. If this is considered a contributory factor towards the problem, your veterinary surgeon should be consulted for possible remedial hormone treatment or castration.

THE LAGGING DOG

Assuming your dog is perfectly well and is not suffering heat exhaustion for example, then the lagging dog suggests either an extremely lethargic dog or a badly trained dog, where too much compulsion has been induced and a lack of praise stimulation. When trying to correct this behaviour *do not* slow down to the dog's pace as this will cause an even slower speed, eventually ending up with both of you in a stationary mode. Breaking into a jogging speed will kindly motivate your dog. A check should *never* be given to induce a lagging dog to "heel", remember when you check your dog you are telling it off. A lagging dog has done nothing wrong. It simply lacks motivation.

A dog, in effect, works at right angles to its owner. By throwing your shoulder back in order to look back at the dog, the right angle will be altered and effectively keep your dog back even more.

THE ETHICS OF SPIKED COLLARS

It must again be pointed out

LAGGING DOG. If your dog is lagging behind you, do not throw your shoulder back in order to look at him as this will keep him back even more. A dog works at right angles to his owner and by moving your shoulder back you are altering the right angle. Illustration by G. Horn.

that the definition "spiked collar" is no more true than the definition "choke chain". Inasmuch as we do not choke our dogs on a chain, neither does a spiked collar pierce the dog's skin. The concept of such collars is that upon the dog's pulling the prongs are forced together causing a pinching sensation on the dog's skin. Import of these items in the U.K. is strictly prohibited, although such items are widely used on the European continent. While not prohibited in the U.S., such collars are frowned upon by many dog people.

The ethics of using such equipment can only be a subject of the owner's feelings and the severity of the problem.

THE NON-SITTER

Higher levels of compulsion or alternative methods are not readily available or acceptable for this exercise. Should your dog show great reluctance and stubbornness when being told to "sit", it is quite likely that he is suffering from a hip or arthritic condition. The German Shepherd Dog breed for example, where hip dysplasia is quite common, is often accused of sluggish response where in fact the poor creatures may be suffering from acute pain or discomfort. If in doubt—check it out.

DIFFICULTY WITH STAY

Again—no short cuts. The dominant dog will require more time, more firmness and more perseverance.

THE "I'LL COME BACK WHEN I'M READY" DOG!

How many owners have read all the books, watched TV programmes and attended training classes but still can't get their dog to come readily when called? If you have such a problem, you're not alone. This is probably one of the most common problems dealt with by professional trainers.

THE "CATCH ME IF YOU CAN" DOG

Such a behavioural problem may well have started when your dog was a puppy heightened by his delight in being chased by you to get it back. This type of dog will typically run back near to you but avoid you at the last moment, normally at high speed. This category of problem is probably the easiest to deal with. It is essential that you stand your ground, as running after the dog will exacerbate the problem. A method of compulsion must now be sought to induce the dog's return. Purchase a small light-weight check chain such as would be suitable for a Chihuahua. Call your dog. As he runs towards you encourage him, but as soon as he veers off course or starts to circle you, lob the check chain at his body and reinforce the "come" command. A positive reaction will be observed. Should he just stop, reinforce the command again and hold the chain aloft in a somewhat threatening manner. Immediately, as the dog comes towards you, all threatening actions should cease and be replaced by copious encouragement. Many trainers advocate a tin containing stones, mainly used as an "attention-getter", but we feel such a projectile to be dangerous or if simply rattled, tantamount to useless. Expensive alternatives such as discs may prove useful, but will not do any greater good than the small check chain. Owners will find that later on a simple jangling of the normal check chain will suffice to help enforce your dog's return.

THE "GIVE ME A COUPLE OF HOURS AND I'LL COME BACK" DOG

Clearly such methods as lobbing the check chain will be totally ineffective for the dog who remains at a longer distance. Despite all conventional training, these dogs will turn a deaf ear to commands to "come" whether said harshly, pleadingly or lovingly. It is necessary, therefore, to use a stronger method of compulsion and enlist the aid of modern technology. Radio-controlled electronic shock collars have proved an enormous aid to trainers in recent years. Such devices used sensitively will induce no more discomfort to the dog than a check or a smack and are profoundly more kind than allowing your dog to stray, endangering himself and others. But the emphasis must be on kindness and sensitivity and ideally the device should be used by professionals or owners should be taught the correct use by professional trainers or behaviourists. Ideally the reaction of the dog to such collars should be checked in a controlled environment such as a confined area or with the dog on a long leash. This is in case he is found to have an adverse reaction to this stimulation or, conversely, the equipment needs to be set higher to induce an effect.

Once the correct stimulation level and response is effected, the dog may now be taken to an open area. The dog is firstly called as normal, "Bonzo, come". Should Bonzo then come towards you, of course the collar under no circumstances should be activated. If, however, the dog does not respond to your command, a further command, "Bonzo, come", should be given more forcibly accompanied with stimulation from the collar. As soon as the dog capitulates, praise him and, of course, lavish affection and pleasure on his return.

THE PANIC SITUATION

Can anything frighten an owner more than the dog hurtling towards a main road, totally disregarding all calls to come back? Theories such as running in the opposite direction to the dog or lying on the ground will indeed encourage a dog towards you, provided he is paying attention and looking at you. If not, these exercises will prove fruitless.

So you have taken your dog out for a walk. He bolts and you are in a crisis. It is now that your training efforts will be rewarded or highlighted as inadequate. A dog running away from you, who makes no reference to you at any time, will simply not recall unless an adequately dominant relationship has been established by you. A significant reaction from the dog, such as turning to observe your position, may well be rewarded by running in the opposite direction to him, thus causing the dog to run towards you or by lying down thereby exciting the dog's natural curiosity to investigate your actions.

THE VERY INDEPENDENT DOG

These dogs pose a real problem to owners and trainers alike for at the end of the day a dog's inherent desire to come back and its wanting of human company will always be a prime motivator for returning. The most useful advice that can be given for this type of dog is to establish a relationship of dependence through conventional training. Nearly all dogs will, at some stage, bond to their owners and become dependent on them. With the independent dog, however, this process may take considerably longer and obvious precautions must be taken in order that he does not run off.

THE SEXUALLY MOTIVATED RUNNER

Although this section is dealing with the problems of "recall", the sexually motivated dog may well manifest its behavioural problems under the escape artist heading and indeed may well manifest itself in both problems. Determination as to whether this is the true cause of the problem should first be established, castration should not be the front line answer as misdiagnosis is irreparable.

ON THE RUN. It is important to establish sexual motivation as the reason for your dog's running off before taking any drastic measures, such as castration. Photo by R. Hutchings.

DOGGONE. The English Springer Spaniel has an inherent desire to put his nose to the ground and go wherever it leads him. Photo by R. Hutchings.

If this cause is considered likely then a course of hormone treatment combined with training therapy will establish positively long-term solutions.

THE "NOSE DOWN AND GONE" DOG

Many breeds, in particular we would cite the Springer Spaniel, put their nose down on the ground, start tracking and just go wherever their nose takes them, regardless of your demands to return. This is, of course, a genetically inherited trait and can pose a real headache to its owner. Although suggestions such as "a peg on the nose" have been mooted, a simpler course of action is more relevant! Try, if possible, to use your dog's natural ability and talent with retrieving throw-bags and working him in field-trial exercises.

Does your dog have a stimulating, active and rewarding life style? If not, perhaps this is why your dog is not coming back to you. If these criteria are filled, then try the aforementioned training methods or seek professional help. Do not feel embarrassed, do not feel you have failed, for there are an extraordinary number of people in the same situation, many saying "I have had lots of dogs, none have done this". But every dog is different (thank goodness) and the art of good training is to work on and mould those differences into acceptable behavioural patterns.

Who's the Boss in Your House?

Does your dog grumble at you when you try to remove him from his favourite sleeping place (the settee)? Does your dog push his way through the door in order that he gets there first, wherever "there" may be, before you?

Does your dog take *you* for a walk and come back only when *he* is ready?

Or is your dog the nice, biddable soul who only sleeps at your feet, or in his bed, displays the manners of a courtier, always allowing you to go first, walks meekly beside you and comes immediately when called?

If your dog is of the former type, he probably sees himself as the boss—top dog—pack leader—alpha or whatever fancy handle you care to give it. However the problem is still the same and he is probably a pain in the rear end!

THE DOMINANCE/SUBORDINANCE DIMENSION: WHO'S IN CHARGE OF WHOM?

In many respects dogs are like us.

WHO'S THE BOSS? It is important to establish yourself as the leader of the pack early on in your dog's life or else you will have "big" problems once he is an adult. Photo by Graeme of Eastbourne.

BORN LEADERS. In order to correct your dog's dominant behavior, do not allow him on the furniture—puppy or adult dog. Photo by Graeme of Eastbourne.

There are those born to be leaders, those born to be led, and those upon whom leadership is thrust.

THE BORN LEADER

This dog was born with dominant tendencies (hereditary) and will need to be singled out early in his life and subordinated in a kind but positive fashion should you not wish such a dog to rule your life.

For as time goes on the problem will not get better unless corrected, but may well get steadily worse until out of control and un-alterable. There are two approaches to correct this behaviour.

1) The behaviourist may suggest:
   a) always going through a door before your dog.
   b) not allowing your dog on the furniture.
   c) not letting the dog assume a height above yours.
   d) feeding your dog after yourself and the family.

But such measures will probably only have a minimal effect, far better that these things be done in combination with the effects of positive training.

2) The trainer may suggest:
   a) Teaching your dog to walk to heel as possibly the easiest and most positive way to subordinate your dog, establishing who the boss is.

BORN TO BE LED. Although owners with biddable dogs experience few problems, a degree of firmness is still needed to ensure this security. Photo by Graeme of Eastbourne.

Many owners of small dogs see little need for such training, after all if they pull, "so what?" But the knock-on effect of the positive approach will be to produce a dog of a far more biddable, overall nature.

b) The "left-about turn" exercise, which requires the dog to walk backwards, produces a submissive reaction.

c) The "flat" exercise may assume little importance to the apartment dweller with a Yorkshire Terrier. But he will, in fact, reap many benefits from this, the most submissive of all exercises from the dog's point of view. This exercise will be the most difficult to teach the dominant dog who may react to such a request with an ill-tempered response.

In conclusion, whether using

the behaviourist's, trainer's or both approaches, dominant dogs will need to be subordinated to conform to our requirements.

THOSE BORN TO BE LED

Most owners will experience little or no problems with this category of dog, although the dog will need a degree of firmness to ensure its security and is more likely to exhibit anxiety problems.

This type of dog will generally respond well to the normal standard biddable-type training. I bet you're glad if your dog fits this description!

THOSE UPON WHOM LEADERSHIP IS THRUST

A naturally submissive dog with a weak owner who allows the dog complete carte-blanche is the worst possible combination. The dog who has become boss doesn't particularly like it, but feels one of them must take charge.

What a shame, when a little training and a few simple dos and don'ts would have prevented such a character from developing.

THOSE UPON WHOM LEADERSHIP IS THRUST. Weak owners unite! Photo by Graeme of Eastbourne.

The Problem Dog

It was not many years ago that dogs with behavioural problems and in particular aggressive behaviour would almost certainly have been taken to the veterinary surgeon to be put down. During the early seventies the public became far more aware that these problems could be dealt with and a particular thanks should go to Barbara Woodhouse for her pioneering work in behavioural modification. Professional trainers became far more respected and sought after for help with the difficult dog. In England, the British Institute of Professional Dog Trainers, which had hitherto largely been an organisation involved in Police and Service dogs, expanded to include trainers who dealt with behavioural problems. Since then the "animal behaviourist" has emerged offering academic support to owners. Whilst every effort has been made in this section to give a broad outline of behavioural problems and ways of dealing with them, it is often advantageous to seek professional advice. Cures to problems are relatively straightforward, once the cause is known. However, diagnoses of the true causes can be difficult. For example, many owners consult trainers and behaviourists when their puppies start to bite them believing this to be the start of an aggression problem. This is most improbable and on consultation we are likely to find the dog has a teething problem. Many problems are inexplicably more difficult to diagnose, requiring skill to extrapolate the dog's history and social environment, identify possible medical problems and read the dog's body signals.

An excellent example involved owners of a five-month-old German Shepherd who they thought to be very aggressive both to humans and other dogs. This dog had been restricted to the lead on the request of their veterinary surgeon because of suspected hip problems and therefore not allowed to freely interact with other dogs or humans. Despite this dog's medical problems it was felt that socialisation must begin before the problem got out of hand and the dog posed no threat because of its size. In fact after initial grumbling at older dogs (who took little notice of it), the puppy began to play happily with them and later enjoyed a game with some young children. The sessions were kept short. Had the owner not sought advice at an early stage of the dog's development this problem could have manifested itself into a potential nightmare for its owners. As it happens the exercise did not worsen the hip problem and the dog now lives a full, happy and non-aggressive life.

Arthur, a Great Dane of

somewhat large proportions, terrified his owner when walking on the lead by freezing on the spot and outwardly giving an appearance of hostility towards other dogs. Because of this the owner was of course reluctant to let him off the lead. The trainer decided that interaction with other dogs off the lead would have to be observed before an accurate assessment could be made. To this end a very expensive king-size muzzle was purchased and, on the day the dog was kitted up with this, an electric collar and a personal attack alarm were also placed on him should a confrontation ensue. In fact, Arthur proved to

FRIENDS FOREVER. Socialise your dog with other dogs known to be friendly in order to establish a positive association of other dogs in your dog's mind. Photo by R. Smith.

have a most delightful disposition with other dogs and enjoyed his free runs enormously. Arthur was still biting at her arm when excited on seeing other dogs, and she was told to be more dominant over him. Nothing changed for a couple of months until one incident caused the owner to become very angry with him at which point she turned round and smacked him in the face. Whilst this practice cannot be recommended, we all have a limited tolerance level and do things we may later regret, but in this case such treatment put a complete end to Arthur's problems. He is now being shown very successfully at competition level and is enjoying a full, normal and healthy life. Well done both of you!

AGGRESSIVE DOGS

Konrad Lorenz in his book *On Aggression* states, "We find that aggression, far from being the diabolical, destructive principle that classical psychoanalysis makes it out to be, is really an essential part of the life-preserving organisation of instincts. Though by accident it may function in the wrong way and cause destruction, the same is true of practically any functional part of any system."

Whilst the examples in the previous section are given to highlight the problem of owner-diagnosis, many aggression problems are of a far more serious and complex nature. Reasons and examples of aggression and suggested remedies are as follows.

If all reasons for aggression and cures were known, there would surely be no one in prison or mental institutions. Whilst the success rate with dogs is somewhat better than that with their human counterparts, knowledge of this subject is still limited.

MENTAL ILLNESS AS A CAUSE OF AGGRESSION

Sometimes known as rage syndrome or more closely akin to schizophrenia, a dog who will normally interact well with humans and other dogs may suddenly and for no apparent reason go into a rage and attack. Such an example was when a Cocker Spaniel, who was happily lying by its owner's feet, suddenly jumped up and severely bit its owner's nose. This type of occurrence must be the most horrific experience an owner can suffer, but fortunately mental illness in dogs is very rare and in most cases identified by the veterinary surgeon at an early age. Most owners of such dogs report physical changes in the animal, in particular colour changes in the retinal reflections.

Before making any hasty decisions as to your dog's future, first consult your veterinarian who may suggest the use of drugs such as Diazepam, or in some cases anti-convulsive treatments have been used to good effect. Regrettably the success rate is limited and inevitably in some cases the dog may have to be put to sleep.

BRAIN TUMOURS AS A CAUSE OF AGGRESSION

Symptoms can be similar to those of rage syndrome although of aggression in the male dog is caused by the male hormone testosterone. Medical research suggests that this hormone

MAD DOG. There are many causes of aggression in dogs, such as mental illness, hormones and fears. Consult your veterinarian or trainer/behaviourist if your dog is acting aggressively. Photo by K. Taylor.

this condition would generally be expected to occur in the older dog. If in any doubt about progressive behavioural degeneration, consult your veterinarian. He may suggest that your dog has a brain scan (if facilities are available).

MALE HORMONE-RELATED AGGRESSION

Perhaps the most common form creates a protein, Amine, in the brain suspected as being the chemical link to aggression.

Observation of this type of aggression shows that flare-ups are slow to abate even when the source is separated, dogs pulled apart after a confrontation for example.

Should hormonal aggression be suspected, a course of hormone treatment such as Ovarid/ Ovaban (Megestrol Acetate) should be administered in preference to immediate castration. Administering of this drug by a veterinarian combined with observation of its effect and suitable correctional training can produce spectacular results. This does not necessarily mean, however, that the same degree of success will be achieved by castrating the dog. It is widely debated as to whether long-term use of hormone treatment, such as Megestrol Acetate, produces undesirable side effects. International drug regulatory bodies offer no such evidence. It would therefore be advantageous after the proving stage to castrate the dog, although continuing hormone treatment should be administered for a further short period until the hormone levels are stabilised.

It must of course be clear that what may start off as a chemical reaction in the dog will quickly be established as a behavioural pattern in the mind and this type of medical treatment will be limited in success if not combined with the correct behavioural modification training.

It is also evident that the chemical effects of hormone treatments are somewhat different from that of castration and successful use of such medication does not necessarily mean the same level of success with castration alone.

Documentation shows a small

HANDS OFF! *Schutzhund* or sleeve work was developed in Germany to train professional guard dogs. This method is not advisable for household dogs. Photo by R. Pearcy.

percentage of dogs in which castration has exacerbated the dog's aggressive tendencies, another good reason why hormone treatments should be tried first as an "indicator".

Some tumours are known to have the effect of increasing hormone levels and many older dogs may suddenly display hormonal aggression tendencies despite earlier castration. Even under such contradictory circumstances hormone treatment may be administered successfully.

FEMALE HORMONE-RELATED AGGRESSION

Whilst aggression in women before periods (P.M.T.) is now well recognised by the medical profession and even the legal profession, little or no understanding has been given to bitches suffering from a similar syndrome during oestrus. Bitches will commonly display character changes before seasons or during phantom pregnancies, sometimes of an aggressive nature. Owners should be aware of such possibilities and not jump to conclusions that their dog's character is becoming unstable. Clearly as bitches are only in season every six months and a large number of owners will have their dogs spayed after their first season, this problem poses minimal difficulty as opposed to more predominant aggression problems. However, many bitches after spaying lose bladder control and in order to correct this malfunction, are prescribed

synthetic oestrogen medication which can produce a permanent P.M.T. effect.

A common cause of hormone aggression in bitches derives from a hormonal imbalance, an excellent example of such being a nine-month-old crossbreed called Amber.

Her owner complained that the dog would bite members of the family should things be taken from her, and that she chewed the carpet when left and barked continually from 5 p.m. onwards. Her disposition towards the owner's husband was extremely violent. We believed after lengthy consultation that the bitch had a hormonal imbalance that would, in part, be sorted out after having her first season. The poor owners waited three months for this occurrence, often phoning for reassurance that the problem would subside. After her season the problems abated considerably. Amber was spayed and other physical hormonal problems became evident causing the veterinary surgeon to administer a short dose of hormonal correction treatment. Amber and her owners now live a full and harmonious life together.

NERVOUS AND FEAR-INDUCED AGGRESSION

Success with such dogs must of course depend upon the extent to which the nervousness can be cured. Observation of the nervous dog will show definitive body signals best analysed by the professional trainer/behaviourist.

The first action should be to

administer medication for the condition. We suggest as an initial action to administer a homoeopathic, herbal treatment or Bach Flower Remedy combined with a specialised diet. This type of treatment has resulted in considerable success with a large number of dogs. However, as with humans, a definitive answer to nervousness has not yet been found. Administering tranquilisers, except in all but the most serious of conditions, has not proved to be a successful course of action and a catapult effect has often been observed on stopping use of the drug and, as with humans, dependency can often occur. This treatment must now be combined with sympathetic and skilled handling of the dog. However a definition of "sympathetic" in this instance does not imply being too soft, as one of the more extraordinary aspects of such animals is that firm handling will produce a more confident dog who feels reassured by the positiveness of its owner. The dog should now be socialised with dogs known to be friendly over a lengthy period in order to establish a happy association in the dog's mind. In the case of aggression towards humans, careful and firm handling must be administered ideally by experienced handlers and the use of food in this situation is encouraged as being a good catalyst.

For example, a German Shepherd Dog, Oliver, was showing hostility to people coming towards him. This was a cocktail problem involving a dominance towards his owners, a little bit of showing off and a large degree of nervousness towards oncomers. A higher level of control was established by the owners with basic obedience training, which caused the showing off and dominance tendencies to abate. Food was used by volunteers when approaching Oliver, who now regards anyone coming towards him as being a great benefactor.

Case two involves yet another German Shepherd Dog called Sieger. This history is particularly disturbing in view of the cackhanded way a class instructor handled the situation, which involved dragging the dog out in front of the class, hauling him up on his check chain and allowing him to dangle in front of the others. This irresponsible and amateurish approach caused the dog to become far more hostile towards people and other dogs. The correctional training therefore involved many hours of patient socialisation combined with firm but kind and sympathetic handling.

Fear induced "by the unknown" is often the reaction of a dog hitherto deprived of socialisation with others. This is commonly found in country areas where regular interaction with others may be rare or non-existent and is an almost unknown phenomenon in urban areas. A carefully planned socialisation programme will almost always yield excellent dividends and if the dog is felt to be highly stressed in these situations, the use of Bach Flower Remedies is recommended. Don't forget that most dogs need the company of other dogs.

PAIN AND ILLNESS

As humans we accept that our bodily condition will have considerable effect on our mental well-being. Prolonged pain may cause us to become irritable and aggressive. The same must be considered true for our animals. Whilst some veterinary conditions may be easily observed, such as hip dysplasia, arthritis and injuries, others may be less obvious, such as stomach pain, tumours and so on. Clearly a dog who has been of a good disposition suddenly showing signs of aggression should be examined by the veterinary surgeon for possible medical causes.

ENJOYMENT OF AGGRESSION

Many dogs simply enjoy the act of being aggressive towards a fellow dog or human being. This is often promoted in their early life by the enjoyment of play-fighting other dogs in the litter, which of course should be discouraged by the responsible breeder. However, many owners also promote aggressive play by playing tug-of-war games and having wrestling matches with their dogs. Again, this should be discouraged. There has been a recent trend to market ropes especially designed for such games. A game with your dog is of course highly desirable, but

should not promote a challenge between him and you. Encourage the nicer and more useful aspects of the dog's character when playing, such as retrieving a ball and playing hide-and-seek games with toys, but always ensure a somewhat reserved position yourself. An owner's mental attitude alone may, of course, promote an aggressive tendency in a dog commonly found with the more aggressive owner who uses his dog as an extension of his own personality.

PROVOCATION

Clearly even the most angelic of dogs will eventually reach a point of provocation where retaliation will ensue. How often do owners require their dogs to be the model of society and yet allow their children free rein to torment the family dog?

How often do neighbours provoke dogs by intentionally leaning over the fence and shouting at the dog in order to quiet it or even hurling projectiles at it? A recent court case involved a dog that lived adjacent to a public house. This dog was continually provoked by drunks and hooligans throwing items at it even to the extent of a paving slab being lobbed into the garden. Obviously this dog became riled and when taken for a walk in a park, nipped a passer-by who was throwing objects around, clearly unaware of the dog's background and without any blame to himself. He of course unintentionally antagonised the dog and sued the owner for damages. This case did have a satisfactory conclusion and on production of evidence to both parties' lawyers to show the dog's due provocation the case was dropped, much to the credit of the aggrieved party.

In a lighter vein, the author has a tale to tell of a dear little mongrel called Judy. Judy had never and would never under normal circumstances, dream of biting a human. However, on this occasion the author's wife was in the hospital giving birth to their son. Dad was staying with his parents, accompanied by Judy, and in order to be helpful decided to vacuum the room, a task seldom carried out by this person! Now unfortunately Judy's tail managed to get caught up in the vacuum cleaner and rather than switch the machine off and disentangle the tail, he decided to lift the machine whilst still running and try to shake her loose with the help of gravity. Needless to say this resulted in this dear little dog turning round and biting his ankle! The aggrieved party did understand her predicament. This was further compounded the following day when slightly confused by the surroundings in which he woke and with a slight hangover from the celebrations the night before, the new Dad got out of his bed and stepped on the poor dog, who proceeded again to turn round and nip him! It must be said that no offence was intended and none taken.

FAMILY TRAUMAS

Perhaps the most adorable factor with our dogs is their sensitivity and their empathy with our moods. Many people have tried to describe this trait as controversial in nature as extrasensory perception. Whatever your view is, it cannot be denied that their understanding of our emotional well-being is deep and profound.

It is therefore not surprising that during traumatic periods in their life, such as the marriage break-up of their owners, illness or death, cause a reaction, sometimes an aggressive one, in such stressful situations for the dogs. Of course, positive help cannot be given in such circumstances except to isolate the dog from such trauma. Avoid arguing in front of your dog as much as you would in front of your children. Remember your dog has very deep feelings also. A dog's bereavement for a loved one will only be healed by the process of time.

THE PROTECTIVE INSTINCT

Apart from the friendship and love that dogs give, one of their most endearing features must be their protectiveness towards us. This trait has been encouraged by humans since dogs were first domesticated. One of the prime reasons for owning a dog is that of personal protection and security, according to James Serpell, Ph.D. of the Companion Animal Research Group, Cambridge University, U.K. It is not surprising therefore that we

BASIC INSTINCT. The German Shepherd has a highly protective nature and for this breed obedience training is of the utmost importance. Photo by R. Hutchings.

have encouraged and developed the guarding instinct in our animals. The dog may be protective towards humans (family), territory or other dogs. Although many breeds display guard-dog characteristics, there can be no better example than that of the German Shepherd Dog whose behaviour, whilst often resembling other forms of aggression, may be purely that of a highly protective nature. Such traits cannot be stopped. The depth of hereditary knowledge is just too profound to tackle. Our only course of action is to acquire a high degree of control through obedience training. The postman often bears the brunt of such protectiveness, after all it is a situation where the dog always thinks he has won. In fact 7,000 postmen, or one in ten, suffer dog bites each year in the U.K. postal service.

The postman arrives, the dog barks and, after delivering the mail, he promptly leaves. The dog sees this as a daily ongoing victory. Try to introduce your puppy from an the community dogs now see the postmen as great benefactors and, instead of exhibiting hostile or protective behaviour, show extreme delight at their arrival.

MACHISMO. Many owners promote aggressive behaviour in their dogs. This is highly discouraged as it can make an already aggressive dog become unmanageable or overly dominant. Photo by R. Hutchings; posed by model.

early age to such visitors. It can help enormously. In a small village in Sussex, England, the postmen have made it their duty to carry titbits to give to their clients' dogs. This has proved very successful as

THE BAD-TEMPERED DOG

Of all forms of aggression, in ourselves and our dogs, a bad temper must be the least understood. Why people from the same social background, similar work, similar family life and similar physical abilities can possess such different personalities (one being of even temper, the other extremely angry and aggressive in personality) is one of the great mysteries of the universe. This is surely as much the case with our dogs, although fortunately the bad-tempered dog is few in number compared with its human counterpart!

FOOD-INDUCED AGGRESSION

A problem commonly encountered by owners is aggression exhibited by the dog when a human or other dog is approaching its food bowl. We may find this particularly strange as humans as we have given them the food in the first place. However, this is not the dog's understanding of the situation as some dogs will perceive approaches to their food as a threat. This behavioural quirk normally begins at an early age through bad husbandry where communal food bowls are put down on a first-come-first-serve basis and a survival of the fittest develops in the litter-environment.

It will do no good merely chastising our dogs for such hostility as the survival for food instinct is of paramount importance in their genetic make-up. We must therefore re-educate them to believe that a human coming towards the food bowl results in additional food, not less. We begin the procedure by putting down an empty bowl or one with very little food in it. The dog will eat the food and look for more. Our hand now comes towards the bowl holding more food that the dog proceeds to eat and he then looks for more. The exercise is repeated until the dog's normal dietary input has been given. However in the early stages do protect yourself by holding the dog's collar and, if necessary, wearing protective clothing such as gloves. This may appear to be a lot of hassle and many owners cannot understand why they should put up with such behaviour or make the effort to correct it, but we must assure you that the results with this type of therapy can be extremely successful.

In the case of inter-dog food-motivated aggression, the only reasonable course of action must be to separate their feeding areas.

CAN A DOG'S DIET AFFECT HIS AGGRESSIVE TENDENCY?

A recent study including video documentary evidence showed a man who, on eating potatoes, became violent and in fact killed two people whilst being under the influence of such an innocuous substance.

Many veterinarians, trainers and behaviourists feel that behaviour can be affected by diet and that some foods can stimulate aggression in vulnerable dogs. Red meat and certain proprietary food additives have particularly caught their attention. There is no doubt some items in food can be connected with over-activity and behavioural problems in children.

Medics at the world-renowned Hospital for Sick Children, Great Ormond Street, London, have studied this carefully by taking such problem children back to a very basic diet and then gradually bringing in other foods one by one to judge any effect. Certainly there is no clear-cut simple ingredient that can be blamed in the vast majority of cases. Most who react badly to certain items also have general allergic states such as asthma, eczema or migraines. For the others there was seldom any single factor and many items in food would upset them, including sugar and protein constituents as well as colouring or other food additives. Equally unlikely is any single factor in dogs. No doubt feeding raw meat increases the hunting instincts of the hound—as well as increasing their risk of tapeworm and other infestation. Overall diet seems an unlikely cause of sudden violence but has to be considered as a factor in aggressive behavioural problems and the owner has to judge this by trial and error with advice from his veterinarian and trainer/behaviourist. A food reaction such as this would be impossible to define in an animal as time and expense would be involved for such research, which in many people's minds would not be warranted. Certain blanket statements therefore have to be made about food and its effect on behaviour. This, of course, does not appertain to a vast majority of dogs who, like human beings, can eat almost anything without reaction. However, dietary changes should be considered for a dog with an aggression problem. Red meats, for example, have long been suspected by some veterinarians, trainers and behaviourists of promoting aggressive tendencies. An example of the proverbial "chicken or egg" situation may be cited. Does the predator, such as the lion, feed on the red meat thus propagating his tendency to further hunt due to his heightened aggression caused by the meat?

Certain additives in some proprietary foods may have the same effect on your dog as in your child. Colourants such as tartrazine have long been shown to have an adverse effect on some children. There is no reason to assume therefore that the same effect will not be true with our dogs. In fact many hyperactive dogs benefit greatly from a dietary change. With your veterinarian's approval, why not try your dog on a white rice and fish/white rice and chicken diet for a month and observe any desirable changes? If this works, you and your veterinarian may, by a careful programme of re-introducing other foods, be able to establish the dietary cause of your dog's hyperactivity or aggression.

Many premium dog foods are now available, offering excellent nutrition but excluding unnecessary additives or red-meat content. This may cause confusion to the believers that dogs are carnivorous by nature. It is more academically accepted

SAFE IN YOUR ARMS. The German Shepherd makes a gentle and loving companion as well as a superb watchdog. Photo by R. Pearcy.

that domesticated dogs are in fact omnivores.

THE WORRY THAT MY DOG MAY TURN AGGRESSIVE

For those who are worried that their dogs may, without any suggested history or reasonable provocation, turn aggressive against them or other dogs, be reassured that unless your dog has suffered severe trauma or has developed an unusual medical condition as previously explained, he should be consistently agreeable from puppyhood to old age.

Curbing Your Dog's Instincts

THE SHEEP WORRIER

Whilst chasing cattle and horses may pose a severe threat and, of course, cause injury to the dog, sheep worrying must still be of paramount concern to owners, particularly in the U.K. where many farmers will not hesitate to shoot a dog if caught even playing with sheep, especially during the lambing season. Very often the cure to this problem can be obedience training reaching a high level of "recall" control. A dog, for example, tied to a long leash within a field of sheep may be taught "recall" exercises safely with this heightened distraction. This will also enable the owner/trainer to establish the dog's desire level and close observation of the dog's body signal should determine whether the dog merely wants to play or is in a serious predatory mood. Whilst this training can be nothing but advantageous it is unlikely to resolve the problem with the

CRYING WOLF. Particularly in the U.K., sheep and other-animal worrying remain big concerns to dog owners. Photo by K. Bing.

PLAY OR PREY. Many farmers in the U.K. will not hesitate to shoot a dog that is caught even playing with sheep. Photo by K. Bing.

serious sheep worrier.

Most authorities agree, be they trainers, behaviourists, shepherds or farmers, that a level of aversion must be created to resolve the problem. Farmers often suggest putting a dog in with rams, who are noted for their hostile behaviour. This will indeed create an aversion towards sheep in many dogs' minds, although it must be pointed out that on occasions this has worsened the situation as some dogs, like some humans, will treat a threat as a challenge. It is also true that many dogs can differentiate between ewes and rams and that serious injury to the dog may result in this exercise being carried out. The help of a skilled shepherd is necessary. Certainly feeding a dog on a staple diet of meat will promote its desire to attack for food. After all, the dog will perceive the smell of sheep as "din-din"! *Do not be confused between the true predatory dog and the one that simply enjoys a game of chase.*

Again the use of modern technology can have an enormous role to play, the electronic shock collar being used as either command reinforcement or as an aversion technique. Considerable successes have been achieved with this medium. However, the dog must first be tested on the leash to observe whether the compulsion, the shock, outweighs the desire as some dogs completely blank out when hunting. An example is a Springer Spaniel, Jessie, who resided on a pheasant farm in Hertfordshire, England. She took it into her mind at a young age to chase and kill as many pheasants as she could. With the aid of an electric shock collar, after just two sessions of therapy, combined with normal obedience training, the dog now in her old age has never reverted to her previously undesirable behaviour.

A particularly difficult problem involved a dog who lived in a house surrounded by sheep. In this instance the electric collar was used both as a reinforcemont for handler's commands and as an aversion therapy technique. Interestingly enough, during the training period, a local farmer offered to put the dog in with his rams. On leaving the shed the dog, despite being terrified of the rams, proceeded to chase the sheep. The owner told the dog to "leave" and had an immediate, positive response from the dog

FIGHTING LIKE CATS AND DOGS. A not-so-dangerous Staffordshire Bull Terrier spending time with the family cat.

thus demonstrating in this instance the lack of success with the rams and success with more sophisticated training techniques. A different aspect of this situation occurred when a lady rescued a mongrel only to find that it did not enjoy the company of her pet rabbit and duck. When advised that the animals needed time to get along with each other and to be slowly introduced, the lady questioned how long this would take. The reply was six months. At five and a half months the lady phoned, delighted to report that they were all living harmoniously, so in this case time was the catalyst.

DOG-EAT-DOG: THE FEUDING SYNDROME

All too often owners introduce a second dog into the family home only to find that one of the dogs takes over a dominant role, often manifesting itself in aggression. Can we help with such a problem?

Direct intervention in these cases rarely works and controversy reigns supreme on this subject. Many trainers and behaviourists suggest dominating the dominant dog whilst many others suggest this is completely wrong and that the dominant dog must retain its status.

It is our belief that the dogs themselves must sort out their ranking and status. How often has a mother tried to intervene when her child is being bullied at school, only to find that she has in fact intensified the problem?

It is however essential under

these circumstances that the humans within the pack (the family) obtain the highest rank by means of positive training and correction. This will effectively lower the pecking order of the two dogs struggling for power. They are therefore far less likely to bother about gaining supremacy for number four or five in the pack than they would in trying to obtain the position of number one.

HOSTILITY TOWARDS OTHER ANIMALS IN THE HOME

It is well documented that dogs brought up with other animals from a very early age will become friends with them, and rarely show hostility. This of course is often not the case when a dog is introduced into a home where animals are already present or conversely where animals are introduced to a home where the dog is already present.

It may reasonably be expected under such circumstances that a period of about six months of gradually and safely introducing the dogs to the other animals will eventually create a mutual understanding between them. Let time be the healing catalyst.

THE ESCAPE ARTIST

This is a disturbing phenomenon to the owner who cannot understand why, after feeding, housing and walking the dog, it still has a yen for the wild, blue yonder. First we must establish if the dog is adequately stimulated. If he is left for considerable periods, maybe eight

UNDER...For the burrowing dog the electronic cattle fence or the "invisible fence" may be in order. Photo by K. Bing.

hours a day, is then greeted by phrases such as "get down, boy" on the owner's arrival home and is not taken out for a walk until the weekend, it is quite understandable for such a dog to become bored and frustrated and look for a life of its own beyond the confinements of its home. Perhaps in these circumstances the dog may have been better off in another home.

If these criteria are not applicable and the dog still wishes for an independent life, this is not a trait that can be modified other than by allowing the process of time and training to form a closer bond and dependency and of course ensuring the perimeter security of your home. Obviously the most normal provision would be that of adequate fencing or walling, but very often people will find the solution unacceptable in terms of aesthetics, cost   and ineffective for the burrowing dog. Electric cattle fencing can be used to good effect, clearly operating at a suitably low, safe voltage. Often such devices can be disconnected, the wire, normally orange in colour, maintained as an indicator for the dog not to proceed beyond it. Modern technology, however, has moved yet another pace forward and can now offer the "invisible fence".

THE DESTRUCTIVE DOG

Close similarities between certain categories of the escape artist and the destructive dog can be drawn in respect of its environmental condition. Again if the dog is not left for excessive periods or is not lacking in mental stimulation, then the problem must be tackled in a positive way.

Anxiety can often be a possible cause of this type of behaviour. The dog has had constant company since being brought home and suddenly finds its human mother having to go to work. This will create anxiety and boredom that can lead to the onset of destructive tendencies. Recent scientific evidence suggests that most damage is caused in the first 15 minutes of the dog being left and on some occasions up to half an hour before the anticipated arrival home of the owner. On leaving the dog, try to detach yourself. Do not bend over the dog making a big

...AND OVER. If your dog is going to great lengths to escape, establish whether or not he is adequately stimulated at home. Photo by K. Bing.

fuss, uttering such phrases as "I'm sorry I have to leave you, old boy". This may well be your feeling and it is to be expected from a compassionate dog owner. But for this type of dog such emotional stimulation will only create deeper anxiety within the dog's mind. Combined with detachment, a diversionary stimulus such as stuffing a hollow marrow bone with grated cheese will cause the dog to spend many happy hours trying to obtain the contents. On arrival home, encourage your dog to fetch a favourite toy. The anxious dog, rather than causing destruction before you arrive, will fondle the toy in anticipation.

Homoeopathy has proved to relieve such anxiety and can aid speedy progress with this problem.

Some dogs, however, show considerably more determination to be destructive. As with all problems of this type, the ideal solution is to catch the dog in the act and chastise it. Setting up such a situation by leaving the house and creeping back to a suitable view point should be effective providing the owner uses enough stealth. Technology can progress this method further with the aid of specialised equipment, such as closed-circuit television now used successfully by many trainers and behaviourists. Clearly if this is not available, advantages can still be sought using a video camera to record the moments when your dog is most active in this escapade, giving you a better chance to find a viable solution. Where certain dogs choose a particular destructive path, such as jumping up and stealing from the kitchen work surface, harmless booby traps can be arranged, such as a long sheet of cardboard slightly protruding over the edge of the surface and set up with empty drink-cans so that arrival of the dog's paws on the work surface will cause an avalanche. This of course is not as successful as a CCTV with microphone and speaker, where the dog can be hailed from an apparently empty house with cries of "Leave that alone".

A publican in Sussex, England, had a Great Dane called Baron, who, when left in their accommodation area, would proceed to cause maximum destruction. However, on close scrutiny of the problem, it was found that Baron was not regularly taken on walks because of an extreme pulling problem causing injury to the wife, nor was he let off the lead because of a severe recall problem. This dog, therefore, was totally lacking in the mental stimulation which is important for all dogs, but in particular Great Danes have an enormous requirement for such input. Baron was therefore taught to walk correctly and trained to recall, making it easier and more pleasurable for his owners to give him regular exercise and company of other dogs. In combination with this training a CCTV system was set up with the monitor (TV set) on the bar much to the amusement of the regulars who actually monitored his movements far better than an owner would be able to do on their own! Baron is now happy to be left, although more and more he is allowed into certain areas of the bar because of his more stable behaviour (and popularity with the locals)!

BARKING

Barking falls into two different categories—that which is acceptable to us and that which is not.

This is a difficult lesson for the dog to learn. If the dog is barking in your presence or even worse, at you, an effective method of stopping this is with the aid of a washing-up bottle, suitably cleaned and filled with water. A command "quiet" accompanied with a squirt of water very often deters a repeat performance. These containers are particularly suitable due to their large capacity and their ability to deliver a suitable quantity of water.

An elderly lady who suffered with a severe barking problem from her dog when he was in the car pointed out to the trainer, quite correctly, that turning to squirt him with the water was not commensurate with good driving practice (point taken). It was suggested therefore that another rear washer jet be installed inside the car so that when the dog barked it was merely a matter of pressing a button. However, this was an old car and perhaps this method is not suitable for the owner of a new Ferrari!

At this point it should be emphasised that shouting at a dog in order to quiet it will have a contrary effect and will just become a slanging match between owner and dog. The olfactory collar can offer a ready solution. Alternatively you may chose the electronic version. Unfortunately the latter devices can be prohibitively expensive, although can prove a cheaper alternative to being prosecuted under Noise Abatement Acts!

MESSING
Puppies

It is unreasonable to expect a young puppy of eight to sixteen weeks of age to go through the night and be completely clean. At this age puppies simply don't have adequate bowel and bladder control. Neither is it reasonable to obtain a young puppy if your lifestyle necessitates your leaving them for long periods of time. Although all dogs need the company of humans, it is particularly important for the younger dog and essential if toilet training is to be successful. A puppy will tend to relieve itself after feeding, sleep and exercise. It is therefore desirable to anticipate their requirements. Take them out into the garden with you and on relieving themselves, give them fuss and praise.

Facing page: HIS BARK IS WORSE THAN HIS BITE. A popular method to control your dog's barking is to squirt him with a spray bottle filled with water accompanied by the "quiet" command whenever his barking is unacceptable.

Flat dwellers of course may not have garden facilities but it is likely that a balcony is available. Try laying down a couple of pieces of turf in order that the puppy may very early on associate relieving himself on grass. For hygiene reasons and because unplanted turf will have a short life, this must be changed on a regular basis. If you feel that this is rather a lot of effort, then the logical argument must ensue that the puppy has been brought into an unnatural environment and cannot be expected to relieve itself automatically when outdoors. Remember it was your choice to have a dog in a flat-dwelling environment and nobody would deny you such pleasure, but because you do not have the facilities a house owner would have, you must be prepared to make a greater effort.

Much misunderstanding surrounds the subject of paper training. The object of this training is not to simply lay down a sheet of paper and expect your puppy to miraculously head towards it in the night and relieve itself. Newspaper should be spread all over the floor of the room in which he is to sleep. This should be done from the day the puppy arrives home to 12 weeks of age (minimum). Habit will be formed during this period. Once firmly established, the newspaper can be slowly reduced (say one less piece every third night) starting at the furthest point from the access door, which eventually will become one piece by the door and further on gradually slid underneath the door, which will cause the puppy to signal when wanting to go out. Do not hurry this training. The more steadily you carry out this procedure the more likely the success.

Adults

This can often be a problem that new owners inherit when rescuing a dog where correct puppy training may not have been given or simply that the dog was used to messing in the rescue kennel. Even if your dog is considerably older than the ages mentioned, we would still suggest that you return to puppy training methods initially. Many adult dogs mess simply because they are over-fed and have ill-planned feeding times.

A Dalmatian bitch was regularly messing in the house despite continual company, regular exercise and previously successful puppy training. The behaviourist who was consulted suggested the owner produce an input/output chart, which was duly studied with diligence but to no avail. It was largely by luck during the conversation with the client that it was discovered that she had misread the feeding instructions supplied by the manufacturer and was in fact feeding the dog three times the required daily intake. No wonder she had a problem!

Whilst most pet food manufacturers make every effort to give an accurate daily dietary requirement, some tend to be somewhat overzealous with their estimates, which, of course, must also depend on the dog's lifestyle.

A working collie for example may require considerably more food than the equivalent-sized dog who is only lead-exercised. The amount of main feed should be reduced proportionally by the amount of any titbits given during the day.

A study of your dog's feeding times combined with its exercise periods may be given to your vet for analysis. In an extreme case if a dog was exercised in the early morning, given a meal, left all day, fed again on the owner's return and not exercised again that day, it would be highly likely that the dog would have such a problem. Exercise will of course stimulate bowel movement and by giving the dog a good free run some time after feeding, the dog is extremely likely to relieve itself fully. As a suggestion therefore, if your regular bedtime is say 10:30 p.m., try feeding your dog between 1 and 3 p.m. Allow the food to settle and take your dog for a nice run at 6.30 p.m. or later if possible (daylight permitting). Of course work and other factors may make this suggestion impractical but do try to ensure that your dog does not go to bed on a bloated

I'M FREE! If you have problems with your dog messing, it may be because he is not given the opportunity of a free run. Photo by I. Francais.

stomach.

Similar problems often occur when dogs are not given the opportunity of a free run. This may be due, for example, to a recall problem in which case the root problem is not the messing but the recall and by tackling the one you will solve the other. Very serious messing problems can be dealt with by confinement training, which may be particularly useful to the flat/apartment dweller. This method relies heavily upon the fact that dogs will not mess their own bedding, although a small percentage of dogs will not obey this rule. The dog is taught to sleep in a confined area, such as a transit cage, and is only let out for exercise and relieving itself. In the early days the dog will have to be released hourly and taken to a suitable toileting area. This method was used very successfully for high-rise dwellers in New York where it was impossible, when seeing a dog anxious to relieve himself, to get the dog into the elevator down to street level and to a suitable area in time. Perhaps under these circumstances this method would be considered desirable but in normal circumstances patience and kindness should serve you and your dog better.

Don't forget that when we talk of messing problems we are assuming your dog's bowel movements are normal. Loose motions and diarrhoea cannot easily be controlled by your dog and veterinary advice should be sought should your dog's condition persist. Some foods contain additives such as gluten or soya, which may cause an irritation in certain dogs.

WETTING

Whilst most people will accept that the young puppy or the geriatric dog will suffer from weak bladder control, it is far less sympathetically understood in the young to middle-aged dog. We must draw a comparison at this point to the human counterpart. How often have you travelled in a car along a highway/motorway with a friend or relative as a passenger. Many people travel for hours and do not wish to relieve themselves, others need to stop at every service station. The same differences therefore must be considered true with our dogs. Obviously the water intake will determine the number of occasions a dog will wish to relieve himself and, whilst it is essential to supply adequate water for your dog, a certain degree of controlling intake can be advantageous, particularly at night when only a small amount of water should normally be required. However, this does not apply should very hot conditions prevail.

Dogs on dried dog foods will require more water than those fed on fresh and tinned foods.

Male

Zoologists in the past have assumed that cocking the leg indicated territorial marking. The modern school of thought suggests that the dog is simply

EXERCISE TIME. Your dog's walks and exercise times should coincide with his feeding times. Your dog should never go to bed on a full stomach. Photo by R. Reagan.

leaving his "calling card". This, however, is a condition found only in the male dog and can on occasions be closely akin to hormone levels; often hormone treatment or castration can alleviate the "marking" problem. Good cleansing of areas that your dog has unhappily marked is essential. We suggest you use a proprietary cleansing solution available from your pet shop or veterinary surgeon for the purpose. Do not use ammonia-based products as they produce a similar scent to that of the urine (soda water can prove a useful cleanser).

Bitches

Whilst bitches seldom display the same voluntary wetting problem as dogs, it is quite common for the spayed bitch to lose bladder control. Normal medication to stop this problem would be a synthetic hormone treatment but take care. Please consult your veterinary surgeon for advice.

DIGGING

Many dogs enjoy a good dig and why not? After all it is part of their genetic makeup. This may not present much problem to the flat dweller or the house dweller with a dilapidated garden. But for the more conscientious gardener this can certainly be a very undesirable behavioural problem. A satisfactory method to stop digging has not yet been found. We therefore suggest that the only alternative is to channel your dog's energy into digging in a pre-

allocated area. Try making a play pit for your dog and play hide-and-seek games with his toys. You should soon find that the dog will naturally go to this area for its recreational digging and burying of its bones, etc.

FEAR OF THE OUTDOORS (AGORAPHOBIA)

Such dogs are almost always of a general nervous condition, which should be treated by homoeopathic, herbal, Bach Flower or conventional medicine. Time and patience will be rewarded. Take your dog on very short walks, maybe only 50 yards to begin with. Do not try dragging your dog forcibly, rather motivate him by using other members of the family going in front of you and encouraging him and indeed if circumstances should permit, his food could be placed outside further and further away from the front door. If not too embarrassing, the food could be placed along the street, in a friend's garden or house. Try to ensure your dog receives friendly greetings and possibly titbits from passing acquaintances. Remember, be kind and patient but also be firm as this firmness will generate security in the dog's mind.

THE DIZZY HEIGHTS SYNDROME (VERTIGO)

Fortunately this is not a very common problem amongst dogs and anyhow it is unusual to find yourself in a situation where this problem would cause difficulty. However we can recall a

Dobermann called Houli who would think nothing of running upstairs to greet his owners in the morning but was then terrified of coming back down again. It was suggested to the client that modification to his open-plan staircase should be carried out. Estimates for this work in 1985 were in the order of £3,000. The trainer initially suggested an 85 percent chance of success which was raised to 95 percent after repeated phone calls. Thus, work proceeded. Happily, the dog immediately responded showing no more trauma at descending the stairs much to the relief of the trainer who had been waiting anxiously for the result.

JUMPING UP

Imagine a poor dog who has been waiting patiently for his owner to return. Due to natural exuberance the dog jumps up to greet his master only to be yelled at and told to "get down". As you come in the door, kneel down to greet your dog at his level whilst holding his collar in order to gently restrain him. But do greet your dog in a soothing manner. We are more often than not to blame for this habit as dogs, when puppies, are encouraged on to owners' laps and facial contact is encouraged. The dog then grows and we start to discourage them from being on our laps and find the jumping up, which was

"DOWN BOY". Discourage jumping up while your dog is still a pup; for although a puppy jumping up seems adorable, an adult dog doing the same is unacceptable. Photo by R. Smith.

hitherto accepted, not welcome. It is better not to allow this habit to manifest itself in the first place. If, however, it is starting to take a hold then gently pushing down and greeting and fussing only when the dog is on all fours should alleviate this problem. However you may have inherited a dog that has a severe example of this behaviour. It should be possible within the family environment to correct the dog in the gentle way described above. Only if this problem does not abate and if, for example, the dog in question was an Irish Wolfhound or Great Dane should more severe methods be used, such as the bringing up of your knee as the dog leaps up at you so that the dog's chest is landing on your knee and not you kneeing the dog.

This behaviour can, however, become manifestly more serious if the dog is running up to strangers and performing the same aerobatic feat. This kind of action is not kindly welcomed by the unsuspecting public. A lot of street walking, particularly in very busy urban areas, often shows good results. Your dog should be easily controllable on a lead, having already been taught the rudiments of "heel" work, and a check downwards combined with the "down" command should alleviate this behaviour. Dogs soon become bored with strangers particularly in busy town areas where people are generally in a hurry and ignore the dog. This type of training, sometimes referred to as "saturation therapy", can have great effect on dogs who live in remote areas, who meet few strangers and who will naturally be "over the top" when a visitor turns up.

PHOBIAS, FETISHES

As with humans there often appears to be no obvious reason why a particular fear or fetish has taken hold. As with ourselves there is no easy cure for these disorders.

Our main advice is that your dog needs to face his problem; avoiding it will make the situation infinitely worse.

Your dog may, for example, have a particular hang-up about walking past a certain wall. Many people's reactions in this situation are to make a big fuss of the dog and try to encourage him past this wall. This will only exacerbate the problem and encourage the fear. Firmness and a positive approach will almost certainly produce greater dividends. Of course, it is not the intention to produce undue stress on the dog and it may be advantageous to seek professional advice before embarking on such therapy. A fetish, such as bike chasing, may have been initially induced by fear (self protection), such as the desire to chase away a perceived adversary, or it may be simply an irrational, overwhelming desire.

Often such fetishes are genetically based. This is particularly true of the Border Collie whose extreme inherent desire to chase and round up

BUTTER WOULDN'T MELT IN HIS MOUTH but Dobermanns do have an inherent desire to chase.
Photo by R. Smith.

can lead it, if not vented by working sheep, to chasing cars, bikes and joggers or, in the case of Dobermanns, an inherent desire to chase for the sheer fun of it. Success with behavioural modification in this area depends largely on depth of its genetic roots. It would be far more difficult to cure a Border Collie, for example, than a Golden Retriever with the same problem. Use of the electric shock collar should prove a successful method of reinforcing your "leave" and "come" commands but should not be used when the dog is too close to its quarry as the dog may well see this as the initiator of its

discomfort, causing a possible retaliatory reaction. It is again of paramount importance that the dog's psychological make-up is fully understood. An electric shock to the timid dog could have catastrophic results, such as bolting off or creating too great a fear of the subject. The very aggressive dog may well be thrust into a hostile mode. The balanced dog, however, should respond well and in this instance true aversion therapy may be in order.

An unusual fetish was developed by a German Shepherd Dog in Hertfordshire, England, who took to swallowing stones. The veterinary surgeon phoned the trainer, concerned that after three operations to remove the stones another operation would not be possible. Painting the stones with obnoxious substances was both impractical and in this case an insufficient deterrent. The electric collar was therefore used, not to reinforce commands but as a strict aversion technique. Great care had to be taken with the timing of this operation; the results were 100 percent successful.

EATING FAECES

This is a problem that deeply disturbs owners as our perception of such behaviour is that of repugnance. It is not always clear as to the reasons why a dog will eat animal mess or even its own faeces, but the problem can certainly be reduced by giving your dog a good complete dog food that is high in bulk and by feeding a small part of their usual dinner just before a walk to take the "edge" off their appetite. Homoeopathic treatment may be considered to marginally suppress the dog's appetite and herbal remedies used to supplement their nutritional intake. Oral anti-flea drugs have been used under veterinary supervision to make the faeces taste foul to the dog.

Of course in the older dog it cannot be ruled out that such an insatiable appetite is not being caused by a medical condition. It is possible to use the electric shock collar as a form of "aversion therapy" in severe cases, but this needs to be carried out by a suitably qualified and experienced instructor.

Due to the uncertainties of cause, the owner will need to experiment with a number of methods. The success rate is high although there are still some dogs who persist despite the owner's best endeavours.

THE BAD TRAVELLER

Assuming your dog has not had bad travelling experiences, such as a very long journey from breeder to home, and providing its initial journeys are kept short with a nice reward at the end, such as a nice run, it is most likely that your dog does not like travel due to a travel-sickness problem, even if not obvious. There are two types of travel sickness:

Sight Sickness

This is caused by the motion of the eye trying to view fast, passing objects. It can be easily cured if the owner takes time and trouble ensuring that the dog remains lying down in the back of the car. Early puppy training can be advantageous, simply practising the "flat/stay" for short periods while the car is still parked at home. On journeys, enlist the aid of a helper to sit with your dog whilst encouraging him and training him into the flat position.

Motion Sickness

Assuming the dog has learned to lie in the rear of your vehicle

GOING FOR A RIDE. When travelling with your dog, keep journeys short with a reward at the end. If you are travelling far distances, stop often to give your dog a chance to exercise and relieve himself. Photo by I. Francais.

PARK AND SMILE. Some breeds travel better than others. Although this makes a fun picture, it is not a safe way to travel with your dog.

and is not continually looking around, should sickness persist it will be of the "motion-induced" type. Medication is necessary to alleviate these symptoms, available either through your vet, local pet shop or by using human medication if approved by the veterinary surgeon. If you simply want to go on the occasional long journey then products that cause drowsiness would not be a disadvantage, but if you wish to solve this problem permanently then a non-sleep-inducing formula should be sought combined with the therapy of short journeys with happy endings.

THE HYPERACTIVE TRAVELLER

Many dogs become very overexcitable on journeys, anticipating a pleasant encounter to follow. Whilst this reaction is quite normal and cannot easily be quelled, personal safety must be of paramount importance and owners of such dogs should use a suitable vehicle with a dog guard separating driver and dog. Dog harnesses are the safest mode of travel for dog and owner. For the occasional long journey where such behaviour will be intolerable, a tranquiliser from your veterinarian may prove beneficial. There are also many dogs who constantly bark in the car causing considerable distraction to the driver.

THE THIEF AND THE SCAVENGER

A dog who is well bred and well looked after is far less likely to be a scavenger although it must be said that strong hereditary traits do have their role to play. Of course your dog may just be excessively hungry. This could be caused by any of the following reasons:
a) unsatisfactory or unsatisfying diet
b) worm infestation
c) dogs on medication such as steroids
d) dogs with serious illnesses such as cancer
e) side effect of hormone treatment or castration
f) additional food requirement of pregnant bitches
g) boredom
   Having eliminated these

GUESS WHAT I'VE BEEN UP TO...If your dog is somewhat of a scavenger it may be because his diet is unsatisfying or simply that he is bored. Photo by T.B. Chadwick.

factors, it may be necessary to put your dog on a mild appetite suppressant under strict veterinary supervision. A Corgi in Hertfordshire regularly jumped on the work surface in order to obtain food from the cupboards. To correct this problem the trainer suggested the drink-can booby-trap routine. The cans were installed high on the cupboards with a splendidly sophisticated device which, as the dog jumped up, caused them to fall. The owner and trainer left this dog to await the crash. This indeed occurred after a short delay. It was, however, most unfortunate that two of the cans landed on the lady's new ceramic hob causing a somewhat large crack to appear. Fortunately she was good natured about this incident. The moral of this story is check your house insurance before setting up booby traps!

Saturation Therapy

There are many behavioural problems which, instead of facing up to them and dealing with them, owners will tend to avoid. A dog who is apparently exhibiting aggressive tendencies towards visitors, for example, is more often than not shut away in a spare room when people arrive; whereas continued socialisation (carried out safely and correctly) may in fact produce a very positive and rewarding result.

A profound example of this method exists when a dog lives in a home where few visitors are received. This particular type of dog, rather than becoming aggressive towards visitors, will go completely "over the top" when people arrive. This can also result in a severe jumping-up problem.

The owner should, in these circumstances, regularly take the dog for a walk in a busy urban area. One such advantage in towns is that generally people are preoccupied and will not stop to fuss at the dog. At first, of course, this will confuse your dog, who has hitherto always received copious fussing from visitors. In this new environment humans will appear aloof and

IT'S JUST ANOTHER DAY. If your dog becomes overly excited when visitors arrive, try taking him for walks in urban areas so that he becomes "saturated" with people—visitors won't seem like such a big deal anymore. Photo by R. Hutchings.

SOCIALLY ACCEPTABLE. This five-month-old English Setter should have already experienced proper socialisation with humans as well as other dogs. Photo by T. Devey.

disinterested. This, combined with the saturation of people, should soon cure the problem.

Many dogs who appear obsessed at getting to another dog whilst on the lead are often found simply to lack free interaction. These dogs, given the opportunity of a good social life, will quickly become far less interested in other dogs and sometimes positively disinterested while on the lead. In Australia anti-smoking clinics are run with enormous success using such saturation therapy methods. As our knowledge of dogs' behaviour increases perhaps we will find more and more uses for this method of behavioural modification.

Dogs and the Law

by His Honour Judge A.F. Waley, VRD, QC, DL The Judge Advocate of the Fleet

DOGS AND THE LAW IN THE U.K.

(For American readers, variations must be found by consulting your own state laws; the principles will be similar even if the detail is different.)

Dogs, like children, feature in both the civil and the criminal law and, with children and dogs, it's the owners who are responsible for their welfare, care and control. However, in a short look at dogs and the law it becomes obvious that penalties for errant dogs, in slight but marked contrast to those available for wicked children (and there are some!), are restricted to a choice between any combination of the destruction of the dog and/or taking the owner's money or right to possess a dog. To avoid these unpleasant fates it is as well to have a rough knowledge of what the law requires of you as an owner: for most of us, that knowledge does not stretch much beyond the by-law threat that used to be seen suspended from street lamp posts and intended to keep pavements clean!

So we should start at the "awful" end of dog law and get that out of the way. Then we can move on to the problems most of us are more likely to meet; chasing livestock without malice, causing traffic accidents, damaging the neighbour's garden and biting the postman. But first,

what about this: "Every person who suffers to be at large any unmuzzled ferocious dog or urges any dog to attack, worry or put in fear any person or animal ..." No, that is not the latest Dangerous Dogs Act but the Town Police Clauses Act 1847; penalty, fine or 14 days in prison. Or by way of contrast : "Any Court of summary jurisdiction (magistrates—U.K.) may hear a complaint that a dog is dangerous and not kept under proper control and may make an order directing that the owner keep it under proper control or that the dog be destroyed" (Dogs Act 1871 [later amended by the Dangerous Dogs Act 1989]). This latter form of prosecution is still common and the decision may be the subject of an appeal to the Crown Court. Destruction orders are suspended pending appeal. This act may be invoked where a dog injures cattle (Dogs Act 1906), that is "horses, mules, asses, sheep, goats and swine"—some of which the majority of dogs rarely meet today! By the 1953 Dogs (Protection of Livestock) Act, the owner or the person in charge of the dog at the relevant time becomes liable to be fined if the dog offends, but exempt are a police dog, a guide dog, a working gun dog or a pack of hounds, amongst other exceptions. How long the immunity of the last two classes will survive the present vociferous onslaught on field sports is hard to say.

And while we are looking at dangerous and ferocious dogs and coming towards the present, it is worth noticing that Guard Dogs became subject to their own statute in 1975. This imposed a licensing system on guard-dog kennels and prohibited guard dogs from roaming unleashed except when under the direct control of their handlers. There was added a requirement for the placing of notices at the gates of patrolled premises. Breaches of these regulations bring financial penalties upon offending owners.

That historically summarises the important thrust of statute law directed in the main at dogs who are malefactors rather than "accident-prone." But, to come right up to date, the recent much publicised attacks by dogs on children and adults have led first to the Dangerous Dogs Act 1989 and then to its more draconian successor, the Dangerous Dogs Act 1991. The first of these put more teeth into the Magistrates' powers (if that is the right phrase in this context!) to order the destruction of the dog under the Act of 1871. Not only may the court now appoint the executioner but it may also disqualify the owner from having custody of a dog for a specified period.

The 1991 Act was aimed directly at fighting dogs, namely the Pit Bull Terrier and the Japanese Tosa and any other breed that the Secretary of State might find to have similar characteristics. Such animals must always be muzzled in public and may not be sold, exchanged, given away or abandoned, nor may they be allowed to breed. Exit the Pit Bull, the Tosa and now the Dogo Argentino and Fila Brasileiro. Convictions for breaches of the Act may bring imprisonment for up to six months and/or a very substantial fine.

It is worth noting that what constitutes a "Pit Bull Terrier" depends on physical and behavioural characteristics.

The Home Office has provided guidance for U.K. prosecuters: courts must make the final decision, the onus of proof that a dog is *not* a Pit Bull Terrier being on the owner who must give 14 days notice of his intention to challenge the allegation, i.e., in this case the dog is, in effect, assumed guilty until proven innocent — a complete reversal of the normal legal assumption.

Rules for obtaining Exemption Certificates for the specified breeds may be obtained from Chief Officers of Police or District Councils who are obliged to keep a register of such animals in the U.K. *Indeed in the Republic of Ireland restrictions are even more stringent as under the Control of Dogs Act 1986 and subsequent Control of Dogs (Restriction of Certain Dogs) Regulations 1991. The following breeds are listed as dangerous:*

"American Pit Bull Terrier,
Bulldog
Bullmastiff
Dobermann
English Bull Terrier
German Shepherd Dog (Alsatian)

Japanese Akita
Japanese Tosa
Rhodesian Ridgeback
Rottweiler
Staffordshire Bull Terrier,
and every dog of the type
commonly known as a Ban Dog (or
Bandog) and every other strain of
cross-breed or type of dog
described.

*These regulations do not apply
however to dogs kept by the Garda
Siochana and wholly used by a
member of same in the execution of
his duty."* In a way the wheel has
come full circle. Perhaps as the
early 19th-century agricultural
community, particularly
vulnerable to uncontrolled dogs
whether defending or attacking,
has gradually been replaced by
"macho" modern man living in all
too close proximity to his
neighbours and often lacking the
skill to supervise safely his under-
exercised and naturally
temperamental charge, so the 1991
Act became necessary. Certain it
is that there were vociferous
owners who protested about the
restrictions imposed on their
lamb-like pets; but hard cases
have been said to make bad law
and surely the majority of the
public rightly or wrongly shed no
tears at what was hoped to bring
the end of horror stories in the
sensation-loving press involving
disfigurement and even death of
the innocent. Of course that aim
has not been fully achieved but
nothing in this life is perfect.

It is right to add that exceptions
may be made under the Act for
dogs individually registered,
spayed or castrated as
appropriate, permanently bearing
identification and covered by a
policy of insurance complying
with the order of the Secretary of
State, thus becoming perhaps
more of a liability than a pleasure
to their keepers. Contrast those
provisions with the universally
applicable (in the U.K.) provisions
of the Control of Dogs Order 1930
requiring all dogs, except dogs
actually being used for sporting
purposes or for driving sheep or
destroying vermin, while in public
places to wear a collar with the
owner's name and address
attached. Local authorities may
and do add their own regulations
under the Order in particular to
be concerned with dogs at large
between sunset and sunrise.
Philandering collarless dogs
beware—a breach may lead to the
humiliation of seizure and
detention as a "stray dog".

To round off the review of
Governmental control of the
canine world, breeding
establishments (like pet shops
and boarding establishments)
require a local authority license.
The authority is required to
satisfy itself before granting a
license that, amongst other
factors, the accommodation is
suitable, that ventilation,
cleanliness, exercise facilities,
food, drink and bedding are all of
a proper standard and that
disease-control precautions are
adequate. A "breeding
establishment" is defined as one
having more than two bitches for
the purposes of breeding for sale
in any premises including a
private dwelling. These

KEEPING STANDARDS HIGH. Boarding establishments require a local authority licence to ensure that the accommodation complies with the standards and that disease-control precautions are adequate. Photo by T. Linsley.

regulations were laid down in the Breeding of Dogs Act 1973 and fortified in 1991 by additional powers for the Authority to apply to the magistrates court for an entry warrant to search premises suspected of failing to comply with its provisions. Financial penalties and disqualification may be imposed for breaches.

There then in brief is the contribution of the "criminal" law to maintaining the peace and of Parliament to providing protection and minimum welfare in a dog's life. It is the compensation that an owner may be required to pay for the dead sheep, the damaged chattel, the uprooted plants and the torn trousers (or worse still, the scarred limbs) that is now worth consideration as a separate issue, which may arise on its own or in addition to any of what has been dealt with in quasi-criminal courts. The fines may be small, the heartache temporary, but the compensation (damages) may be crippling: the ewe that falls is always the pride of the flock. What dead hen was not the best layer or what torn suit was not a "designer exclusive"? That is "Murphy's Law" of inflated injury. It is important therefore that the dog owner should be aware of the risks and the limitations on his liability.

As in so many other fields of law what used to be governed by the common law interpreted by precedent is now codified, in this case into the Animals Act 1971. Following the old form it divides animals into dangerous and non-dangerous species; for this purpose we can ignore the former save to say that the keeper of such a beast is liable for any damage it does and while that was specifically restricted to "animals not commonly domesticated in the British Islands", it must now surely embrace the dangerous breeds of dogs.

The keeper of a dog, a non-dangerous species, is similarly liable if he should have foreseen that, unrestrained, it was likely to cause damage because of its individual characteristics of which he knew. That is a précis of the relevant section of the Act and, since this is not a text book, if your dog has worrying personality traits that might bring you within the section, do look at it.

It is important, though, to be sure that you understand who is the keeper—"the owner, the person who has it in his possession or the head of the household (these days that might produce interesting litigation!) of which a member under 16 owns the animal or has it in his possession."

Knowledge of the particular animal's characteristics that might lead to it causing damage may lie in the keeper or a person who had at any time had charge of the animal as that keeper's servant (these days, usually an employee) or, if the keeper is head of the household, another keeper in the household under the age of 16.

As drafted, the Act leads to some unexpected results. The keeper remains liable for any damage the dog may do for however long it may be at large, either escaped or abandoned, until it comes into the possession or ownership of another person. On the other hand on the sale of a dog with "mischievous propensities", the vendor who keeps quiet about them ceases to be liable and the purchaser and new keeper does not become liable until he discovers them. There is an unfilled gap when any victim is unprotected.

What then are the kind of characteristics not normally found in the species, or not normally found except at particular times or in particular circumstances that give rise to liability once the keeper has knowledge or imputed knowledge of them? Well, the field is infinite but a couple of examples limited to dogs may help.

If your dog is frightened by traffic when off the lead and, in fear, bolts for shelter whenever free to do so, you would keep it on a lead. If a friend takes the dog out for you, warned by you or not, and unleashed, it careers through the traffic causing an accident you may get a very large bill for repairs. Similarly if your dog cannot stand cyclists or horsemen and always attacks them you may be paying for the hospital, for loss of wages, for pain and suffering, for damaged clothing and even for a new bicycle or horse: but remember, there is legal force in the old saying that every dog is

ON PATROL. As long as you are aware of your city's ordinances regarding dogs in public places, you should experience little or no trouble between your dog and the law. Photo by J. Combe.

allowed one bite. It is once you know that you become liable.

Again if your dog always attacks another who is on a lead and on occasion does so injuring a valuable prize winner (Murphy's Law again), who in trying to escape pulls over his owner who in falling breaks a limb ... Invention could easily produce an increasingly gloomy and expensive scenario but perhaps the message is clear.

Take heart, however, for there are defences to claims for damages arising from the misdemeanours of your dog. Apart from the ordinary common law doctrine of contributory negligence, a keeper may plead against anyone but his servant that the injured party voluntarily took the risk of damage to himself (A warning, "If you do that he will bite you"—"Nonsense, I know how to manage dogs"—snap!).

Further, a trespasser on your land may have no claim against you if attacked by your dog provided, of course, the dog is not an offending guard dog within the Dangerous Dog Act. And "may have no claim" is a sensible way to express it because the definition of trespasser is very narrow and a wide class of persons may claim an implied license to enter a stranger's premises for an innocent purpose. A clear warning of the dog's presence is a wise precaution if it is known to resent visitors.

Trespassers in ordinary parlance may not be trespassers in law.

If the damage is due wholly or partly to the fault of the injured party then the owner or keeper may be relieved of all or part of the liability. Against that, the old defences of "Act of God" (as lightning melted the security chain!) or of showing that the act of a third party led for instance to a dog's escape have disappeared in the new legislation, which aimed to achieve strict liability on the forewarned keeper. In the latter case there may be some hope of success in an action against the third party for the keeper's loss but in the former, none.

In a separate section of the Act, special consideration is given to liability for injury done by dogs to livestock. As anyone who lives in a sheep-farming area knows, your normal friendly family "pooch", either alone or worse still with like-minded companions in a field of sheep, will behave as badly as any ghetto rent-a-mob. Every lambing season brings its tale of ewes harried to death or giving birth to premature stillborn lambs because of the one "mischievous propensity" shared by all too many of the canine race, namely the urge to herd and chase the silly woolly creatures so often to be found unprotected.

Hence Section 3 of the Act— "where a dog causes damage by killing or injuring livestock, any person who is a keeper of the dog is liable for the damage except as otherwise provided"... Obviously there is no requirement for the keeper to know that his dog may cause damage as in the cases considered above. Livestock thus get greater protection than human beings and, where several dogs are involved, the keeper of any one of them may be sued for all the damage created by the dogs together.

Again there are defences: if the livestock stray on to your land you may be immune from liability for what your dog does to them if your fences are in order. And you may escape wholly or in part if you can show that, although not on your land, the damage resulted wholly or in part from the negligence of the owner of the livestock. This should not be regarded as a promising field for endeavour!

It is interesting perhaps to compare the definition of livestock in this Act with that of cattle in the Dogs Act 1906 referred to earlier. Sixty five years on we are dealing with "cattle, horses, asses, mules, hinnies, sheep, pigs, goats, poultry and deer not in the wild state, together with pheasants, partridges and grouse while in captivity." I suspect few owners would recognise a hinnie, which is the offspring of a she-ass by a stallion (Oxford Dictionary), a snippet of knowledge that may or may not come in handy.

Poultry are further defined to include fowl, turkeys, geese, ducks, guinea fowls, pigeons, peacocks and quails. Dogs will be pleased to know that rabbits are altogether excluded.

There is therefore a formidable list of creatures enjoying

substantial statutory protection from your dog who must, as a result, enjoy your careful supervision to prevent your facing the threat of financial ruin.

Outside the provisions of the Act that have been referred to, it remains the case that "every person has a duty to take care that his animal or his chattel is not put to such a use as is likely to injure his neighbour— the ordinary duty to take care in the cases put upon negligence," so said a law lord in a case in 1932, and so it is today.

Thus, damage caused by your dog in your neighbour's garden on one occasion may do no more than strain a friendship. Repeated depredations by an inveterate tunneller may give him a remedy under the Act of 1971 or under the Common Law for "private nuisance". Lawyers do not lack ingenuity in finding grounds for litigation, after all their modest bread and butter depend upon it. Ignorance of the law is no defence and every owner/keeper thus has the heavy burden of the responsibilities I have outlined firmly upon his shoulders.

Parents who read books of advice on the upbringing of children and the dangers attendant on that activity must be left marvelling that so many reach adulthood safely and

BEWARE OF DOG. A clear warning of the dog's presence is a wise precaution. Signs such as this one will alert visitors of a guard dog on duty.

comparatively unscarred. The dog owner too, reading these awful warnings must wonder that so many happily enjoy their pets without being involved in litigation. The plain fact is that with good training and sensible restraint your dog will never drag you into court. Millions of happy owners can testify to that.

Australian Dog Law

The legal requirements of dog owners is very much the same in most parts of the world. The law, however, tends to remain the domain of the legal profession as they are often the only people able to fully understand the legislative jungle, inaccessible to the lay person.

The City of Perth, Western Australia, has produced an exemplary guide, leaving the dog owner in no doubt as to his responsibilities and consequences for his dog's misdemeanours.

Perhaps all authorities should publish a no-nonsense guide like this one issued by the City of Perth.

YOU, YOUR DOG AND THE LAW

A dog gives companionship, loyalty and love. Owning a dog is a privilege, not a right and with that privilege goes the responsibility for proper care and control of your dog and consideration for neighbours and the environment.

CHOOSING YOUR DOG

Select a dog suitable to your family, local environment and housing circumstances—a small dog may be more appropriate. Remember that cute puppies grow up to be adult dogs who still require training, exercise, care and attention. Be aware that cross-breed dogs are more difficult to assess than one of a known breed as regards size and temperament.

REGISTRATION

All dogs over three months of age must be registered. Dogs should be registered with the Australian National Kennel Council where they normally reside. Should you move within the State, you do not have to re-register your dog, but the change of address must be given to the Council where the dog is currently registered. All registrations are due on the first of November each year and run either one year or three years. Upon production of a Pensioner Card, pensioners may register their dogs for half the usual fee.

Registration helps you to recover your dog if he gets lost and assists the Council to encourage responsible dog ownership and provide services to dog owners for the benefit of the whole community. A person under 18 years of age may not lawfully register a dog in his/her name. The dog must be registered by a parent or another adult who will then be regarded as the lawful owner.

MAXIMUM NUMBER OF DOGS

The City of Perth Dog By-Law limits the number of dogs kept on the premises to two dogs over the age of three months and the young of those dogs under that age. A person may apply to Council for an exemption to keep up to six dogs over three months of age or to become an approved kennel establishment.

FENCING REQUIREMENTS

Person wishing to register a dog must make a declaration to certify that the fences and gates at the premises where the dog is kept are capable of confining the dog within those premises. Gates must have effective self-closing mechanisms.

I.D. REGISTRATION TAGS

The dog's registration tag must be attached to the dog's collar. The name and residential address of the owner must also be legibly endorsed or inscribed on or attached to the collar. Should the dog be lost these tags will enable quick identification and notification of the dog's owner.

EXERCISE YOUR DOG

A dog may only be exercised in a public place if it is on a leash, (2 meter maximum length) and held or led by a person capable of controlling that dog.

This requirement does not apply to "Prescribed Exercise Areas" and dogs being exhibited for show or participating in obedience trials and classes. Areas outside the metropolitan area or other built-up areas are also exempt from these requirements. Greyhounds must be muzzled and held on a leash at all times that they are in a public place. Dogs must be under "effective control" in all Prescribed Exercise Areas.

Dogs may be exercised off leash in "Prescribed Exercise Areas", however, a person capable of controlling the dog and liable for the control of the dog must carry a leash capable of being readily attached to control/ restrain the dog. A list of the "Prescribed Exercise Areas" is available from Council's Health Department.

There are limitations on some Free Exercise Areas, e.g., Council-authorized functions and reserve maintenance work—lawn mowing, etc.

DOG ATTACKS

The number of dog attacks is unfortunately increasing. They can vary greatly in the degree of severity. You should be aware that an attack need not involve the dog actually inflicting a wound. Allowing a dog to attack or chase a person, animal or bird owned by or in charge of another person whether or not injury occurs may incur a penalty. This penalty is doubled for urging or setting a dog to attack a person, animal or bird.

NEIGHBORLY MANNERS
Barking

Barking is a dog's natural means of communicating and often signifies its alertness to danger or intruders. However, a dog which persistently barks in a manner which is not considered to be normally habitual in dogs constitutes a nuisance.

If a dog barks continually without reason, the cause may be lack of training, insufficient exercise, loneliness, inadequate shelter, ill health or deliberate or unintentional provocation by people or roaming dogs.

Excreta

Permitting your dog to excrete on a street or public place and failing to remove or adequately dispose of such excreta constitutes an offence under the City of Perth Dog By-Law.

Training

Training your dog is an essential responsibility of owning a dog. Basic dog training is simple. Both you and your dog will benefit from the mutual trust and understanding that training develops. It will also make your dog more socially acceptable.

Euthanasia

Sadly our dogs grow older far more quickly than we do, and it is very rare for them to die in their sleep. The quality of their lives deteriorates as a result of aging and disease, and we have the responsibility of deciding whether it is fair to let them continue. This is an enormous decision, made with great difficulty. It can seem to be a complete contradiction of all the care and love that you have given, to ensure that your dog has a happy, healthy life. In reality, deciding on euthanasia can be the kindest and most loving thing you can do for your pet.

The decision must be based on the quality of your dog's life. Can he eat and drink without vomiting? Can he move about reasonably well and is he free from unreasonable pain? Is he enjoying life? If the answer to any of these questions is no, can he be treated to relieve or cure these problems?

Your best adviser at this time can be your vet. He has the knowledge and, sadly, the experience, to help you reach a correct decision. A veterinarian's job is to prevent and relieve suffering in animals. That is why they do it. Do discuss euthanasia with him. He may be treating your dog already for problems of old age and this may be a good time to talk about the problems and ethics of euthanasia before you are under the stress of actually making a decision. If, at the time, both you and your vet are convinced that euthanasia is right, you can be sure that you are doing the best thing for your pet.

Veterinarians carry out euthanasia by injecting a barbiturate, usually in the vein of the forearm. Depending on the circumstances, another route may be used or a sedative may be given first. Euthanasia is also stressful for your vet. He will want to use the best method available to ensure that your dog is not subjected to distress or discomfort.

Whether you are present at this time is entirely up to you. Some people prefer to be with their animal to the last. Others are worried that their distress will be understood by their dog. It is your decision to do what you think is right. After all, you know and love your dog better than anyone.

COPING WITH THIS SAD TIME

The students at the School of Veterinary Medicine, California University, have set up a support "hot-line" for owners who have suffered the loss of a pet. This scheme has proved an invaluable preparation for the students' future role and enormously helpful for the bereaved. Some of the most distressing moments for a veterinarian and others concerned with animal welfare are when they have to counsel owners faced with this decision in order to avoid any further pain and suffering by their pet. Time is

MY OLD PAL. Lucy, an 11-year-old Cavalier King Charles Spaniel. Photo by M. Stockton and J. Oram.

needed for the owner to adjust.

Many have found support groups with which the owner can be put in touch for individual or group support counseling which can help share their sorrow and ease the pain. Their emotions are deep and many feel guilt at having to make the decision, a small number even react with a suicidal state of depression.

Once the fateful decision has been made, the way euthanasia is carried out can determine how long these reactions last and part of the counseling process is a

A GOLDEN MOMENT. Who can underestimate the human-animal bond? It always pays off to treat your good friends with respect and kindness. Photo by Karen Taylor.

decision on where and how it should take place and who should be present. Many elderly people will return to an empty home, having lost their only companion, without family and friends to support them. Some veterinarians carry out this sad task at the owner's home, some accept that the owner and even the whole family would like to be present with their pet. It is now that the relationship established between the veterinarian and his client is fully realised. Often the veterinarian has formed a deep attachment to the dog and its family and is himself personally involved.

Finally a decision has to be reached as to how and where final burial should take place and any form of memorial that is desired. All these things are important to help attune to the loss of a family member and to many for the decision about accepting another dog in the future. It may never be possible to replace an old friend but a new one will enter your heart in time.

An Animal Blessing

Lord God, Creator of all things,
we give thanks to you
for all those creatures who share with us
this earthly home,
especially our dogs and other pets,
whose companionship and loyalty we cherish.
Bless all that enriches their lives and our own,
and help us to be loving and responsible owners,
through Jesus Christ our Lord. Amen.

His Grace the Archbishop of Canterbury

The Archbishop of Canterbury with his Cavalier King Charles Spaniel, Duke of Buccleuch. Photo by D. Tamea.

Index

All-Breed Dog Books From T.F.H.

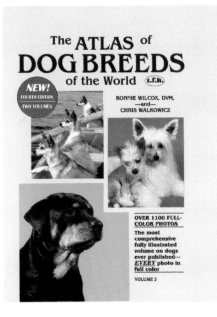

H-1106, 544 pp
Over 400 color photos

H-1091, 2 Vols., 912 pp
Over 1100 color photos

H-175, 896 pp
Over 1300 color photos

The T.F.H. all-breed dog books are the most comprehensive and colorful of all dog books available. The most famous of these recent publications, *The Atlas of Dog Breeds of the World,* written by Dr. Bonnie Wilcox and Chris Walkowicz, is now available as a two-volume set. Now in its fourth edition, the *Atlas* remains one of the most sought-after gift books and reference works in the dog world.

A very successful spinoff of the *Atlas* is the *Mini-Atlas of Dog Breeds,* written by Andrew De Prisco and James B. Johnson. This compact but comprehensive book has been praised and recommended by most national dog publications for its utility and reader-friendliness. It is the true field guide for dog lovers.

Canine Lexicon by the authors of the *Mini-Atlas* is an up-to-date encyclopedic dictionary for the dog person. It is the most complete single volume on the dog ever published, covering more breeds than any other book as well as other relevant topics, including health, showing, training, breeding, anatomy, veterinary terms, and much more. No dog book before has ever offered this many stunning color photographs of all breeds, dog sports, and topics. (over 1300 in full color!).

More Dog Books From T.F.H. Publications, Inc.

H-1106, 224 pp
135 photos

H-969, 224 pp
62 color photos

H-1061, 608 pp
Black/white photos

TS-101, 192 pp
Over 100 photos

SK-044

TW-102, 256 pp
Over 200 photos

TW-113, 256 pp
200 color photos

H-962, 255 pp
Nearly 100 photos

SK-044, 64 pp
Over 50 color photos

PS-872, 240 pp
178 color illustrations

H-1095, 272 pp
Over 160 color illustrations

More Dog Books From T.F.H. Publications, Inc.

KW-156

KW-226

TS-148

KW-177

KW-161

KW-072

KW-175

KW-176

KW-182

Discontinued

KW-010

T-122

CO-032S

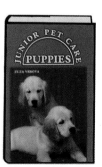

H-1021

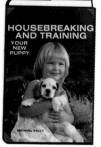

TU-011

PB-123

SK-025

KW-023

J-002

Standard Breed Books and Husbandry Manuals from T.F.H.

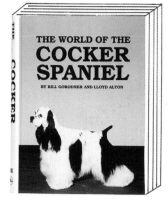

TS-198, 624 pp
Over 1500 Photographs

TS-197, 480 pp
Over 700 Photographs

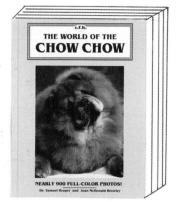

TS-149, 528 pp
Nearly 900 Photographs

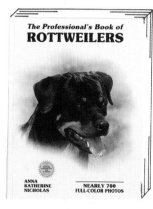

TS-147, 448 pp
Nearly 700 Photographs

TS-176, 304 pp
Over 450 Photographs

TS-187, 224 pp
Over 200 Photographs

TS-196, 352 pp
Over 450 Photographs

TS-143, 256 pp
Over 250 Photographs

TS-150, 224pp
Over 200 Photographs

T.F.H. Publications, Inc. &
The Westminster Kennel Club
Introduce

The First **Official** Yearbook
of America's Premier Dog Show

Every AKC breed described and represented in full-color
photographs of the year's finest champion dogs.